AF859763

To your success!

PRIVATE FUNDS
FOR INVESTMENT ADVISERS

PRIVATE FUNDS
FOR INVESTMENT ADVISERS

HOW TO BECOME A MAGNET FOR HIGH-NET-WORTH AND INSTITUTIONAL INVESTORS

ADAM PONDER

Copyright © 2021 by Alta Trust Company. All rights reserved.

No part of this publication may be reproduced, stored in a retrieval system, or transmitted in any form or by any means, electronic, mechanical, photocopying, recording, scanning or otherwise, without the prior written permission of the author.

Legal Disclaimer: The information provided in this book is for informational purposes only and is not intended to be a source of legal, tax, securities or any other advice or with respect to the material presented. The information and documents contained in this book do not constitute legal, tax, securities or any other advice and should never be used without first consulting with competent professionals such as attorneys and certified public accountants to determine what may be best for your individual needs.

The publisher and the author do not make any guarantee or other promise as to any results that may be obtained from using the content of this book. You should never make any decision as it relates to the material in this book without first consulting with your own attorney and certified public accountant, and conducting your own research and due diligence. To the maximum extent permitted by law, the publisher and the author disclaim any and all liability in the event any information, commentary, analysis, opinions, advice and/or recommendations contained in this book prove to be inaccurate, incomplete or unreliable, or result in any investment or other losses.

Content contained or made available through this book is not intended to and does not constitute legal advice or investment advice and no attorney-client relationship is formed. The publisher and the author are providing this book and its contents on an "as is point-in-time" basis. Your use of the information in this book is at your own risk.

Private Funds for Investment Advisers: How to Become a Magnet for High-Net-Worth and Institutional Investors by Adam Ponder

1. BUSINESS & ECONOMICS / Investments & Securities / General
2. BUSINESS & ECONOMICS / Investments & Securities / Portfolio Management
3. BUSINESS & ECONOMICS / Investments & Securities / Analysis & Trading Strategies
4. BUSINESS & ECONOMICS / Investments & Securities / Real Estate
5. BUSINESS & ECONOMICS / Corporate Finance / Private Equity

ISBN (hardcover): 978-1-7372250-0-3

Edited by Marcy Gardner
Book design by Elena Reznikova

ALTA TRUST

Published by Alta Trust Company, Inc.

For more information or to contact the author, visit TRUSTALTA.COM

To my dad, Mark Ponder,

who taught me all about life first and business second.

I couldn't have done any of it without you.

Contents

Foreword

I MAY INITIALLY SEEM LIKE AN UNUSUAL CANDIDATE TO WRITE THE Foreword for this book. I'm an Assistant Professor of Accounting at the University of Denver and have been in that capacity for the last 6 years. But there are a few legitimate reasons I am qualified to recommend this book to you — and I do highly recommend it.

First, prior to teaching, I spent 20+ years working mostly in the financial services industry at firms including Deloitte, Goldman Sachs, and PIMCO, and 12 of those years were focused exclusively on private funds. I worked for 10 years at Goldman Sachs in its Hedge Fund Administration practice, co-managing two different Goldman offices in New Jersey. I lived and breathed hedge funds every day, working closely with our clients, their investors, their attorneys, their compliance departments, their prime brokers, and their auditors. I have advised funds prior to their launch about proper fee structures; writing an effective LPA or POM; crafting proper investor reporting, subscription, and redemption policies; setting up side-letter agreements; and the list goes on.

Second, after leaving Goldman, I became the CFO of a start-up hedge fund. I experienced firsthand the effort and significant expense required to launch a new fund on our own without a "platform" or "turnkey" solution. How I wish this book had been around at that time and that the Alta Trust Private Fund Program had been available to speed up and simplify our launch process. I can think of several costly mistakes we could have avoided.

Will this book answer every question you have about launching a private fund? No.

Will this book preclude you from doing your own research and hiring competent legal counsel? No.

However, will this book light the way along your path, provide you with new ideas, help you avoid common pitfalls and unnecessary expense, and help make your private fund launch a reality and, more importantly, a success? Absolutely!

I heard it said once that wise people learn from their own mistakes, but super-wise people learn from other people's mistakes. That's essentially the purpose of this book, to help you launch a fund and learn from Adam's own mistakes and successes as well as Alta Trust's experience. In fact, my favorite chapter in the book is called "*The Mistakes Advisers Make and How to Avoid Them.*" Setting up a private fund for the first time without reading this book would be like trying to cross a treacherous jungle on foot without first consulting a map and speaking at length with someone who had already done it successfully. This book will help you avoid making costly mistakes, help you zero in on the proper strategy before getting too far along, will help you understand the complex compliance and legal landscape, and will make your launch go more quickly and much more smoothly. After all, the real benefit of the book is to help you overcome your greatest weakness: you don't know what you don't know.

Another saying is "If you want to be a millionaire, find a millionaire and do what they do." If you want to launch a private fund for the first time, find someone who has already done it and is an expert at it and do what they did and follow their suggestions. Adam and Alta Trust are the experts on this.

I wish you luck along the private fund path!

Sincerely,
A. Tom Hall, CPA, CFA

Introduction

INVESTMENT ADVISERS UNIVERSALLY HAVE A CURSORY KNOWLEDGE of private funds, but very few truly understand them—how they work and how to use them to grow their business. They don't realize that there is a whole world of investing that would be so exciting and rewarding for their clients and themselves if they just took the time to learn about it. I decided to write this book because I see such a wide and consistent knowledge gap within the adviser community. If advisers only knew how private funds could transform their firms into magnets for high-net-worth and institutional investors, they wouldn't hesitate to use them.

Are investment advisers really missing out? It's true, investment advisers are uniquely positioned to make an incredible difference for their clients and for their own families, but instead most count themselves out before they even start. If you are an investment adviser or investment manager, I hope you will catch the vision and enthusiasm that is behind this concept of running your own private fund. Don't count yourself out too soon. Don't give in to the voice in your head saying, "I don't have any experience" or "You have to be really smart to run a hedge fund" or even "I wouldn't even know where to start with private equity or real estate. It's not my thing."

After reading this book, I am confident that you will see how to make it work and how to fill in any gaps in knowledge you may have. You will see how to grow your business in a far more efficient way. You will see why there is so much opportunity in private investments and how you can be a part of it. Keep reading. You won't be disappointed.

What is a private fund? A private fund is a fund that is only available to accredited and other sophisticated investors, and not to the general public. Private funds can invest in virtually anything and have sophisticated fee schedules, including management fees and performance allocations and preferred returns. They are powerful tools that can allow investment advisers to differentiate themselves, serve their clients and reward the investment adviser handsomely.

I speak to advisers every day. Quite often they describe what they want to do and don't even realize that a private fund is what they are looking for. I usually hear statements like, "I don't want a mutual fund, but I do want a way to manage assets for clients all in one account." And "I would like to get paid extra for good performance, but is that even possible?" They typically go on describing the types of investments they want to use and how much their strategy would benefit their clients.

It's rewarding for me to put a name to the type of offering advisers are describing. They are relieved to know that there is such a thing and that it is simpler than they think. Once they know what private funds are, we typically discuss the rules they must follow and the different structures that are available to them. The process continues for a few weeks as we regularly meet to discuss the different fee structures, redemption options and whether to allow the fund to be marketed publicly or to keep it private. Ultimately, they come to just the right structure for their particular vision—and then we bring it to life!

When advisers discover private funds for the first time, I feel like I am helping the blind to see. These are talented professionals who have a desire to give their clients the very best investments. They often feel that there is a way to do what they want, but they don't know where to start or who to trust, and they fear that the expense and risk won't be worth it.

So, how did Alta Trust become the "go-to" for private funds for so many advisers? Originally, my father, Mark, and I owned a registered investment adviser (RIA) ourselves. We served both wealth and retirement clients. As you have probably experienced, many of our clients at the time asked us about real estate or other "alternative" investments that were beyond the scope of our traditional business. We had some very persistent clients and after months of their prodding, we created our first private offering in 2008. We learned a lot during that experience, mostly what not to do!

Fortunately, we also saw the value in offering private funds, so shortly after we launched our first fund, we opened a second. The second fund was a great success and in less than three years, we were able to return the investor's principal along with a return of well over 60% to our investors. Since then, we have shared our expertise and passion for private funds with other investment advisers. We consult with advisers, assist in the fund formation and provide a finely tuned administration, compliance assistance and a robust reporting platform to make sure everything runs smoothly for the adviser. There are so many options when it comes to private funds, and you need a partner who has been there before. We founded Alta Trust 13 years ago so we could take what we had learned as advisers and go to work for advisers to help them launch private funds of their own.

This book is for you if you have ever wanted to provide your clients with investment alternatives that you control, but like most advisers, aren't sure what you can do within a private fund or how to launch one. This book will save you months or even years of wasted time and research, and will easily save you tens and even hundreds of thousands of dollars. More importantly, if you follow the recommendations in this book, you will have the opportunity to make millions of dollars for your firm, all while enriching your clients and investors in life-changing ways.

Note to the Reader

As you read this book, you will see many references that you might find unfamiliar. In the private fund world, there are usually many ways to refer to the same thing. For instance, an investor in a fund may also be referred to as a "limited partner" or "LP." I have tried to remain somewhat consistent in the terms I use for ease of reading; however, I have sprinkled in various synonyms to expose the reader to other common terms as well. I will cover the most common terms in the book, but be aware that there are many variations of the terminology in use. I will define most terms as you read the book, but I want to clarify how I will use a few important terms at the outset.

First, I will use the term "adviser" to mean any person or entity that recommends investments or manages investments directly. Second, I will refer to the creator of a fund as either the "general partner," "GP" or "sponsor." Finally, I will refer to those individuals or entities investing in a fund as "investors," "limited partners" or "LPs" interchangeably.

1

The Private Fund Opportunity

THE FACT THAT YOU ARE READING THIS BOOK TELLS ME THAT YOU are a top adviser or on your way to becoming one. Our industry is full of opportunities for innovative advisers simply because there are so many inferior advisers out there. There are also a lot of good advisers who just want to keep their heads down and do what they have always done because change is hard. This book is for advisers like you, who are open to new ideas, who want to continually improve and expand client offerings. I've packed this book full of the tools advisers need to attract high-net-worth clients and take their firms to the next level.

The Opportunity Most Advisers are Missing

If I were to rank the best opportunities for investment advisers, private funds would be very near the top of the list. Private funds have become an increasingly popular vehicle over the last several decades for high-net-worth investors, family offices, pensions, endowments and other institutions to put their money to work. Most traditional investment advisers shy away from using private funds in their client portfolios. In fact, according to MarketWatch, only 14% of advisers recommended private investments to their clients last year.

I am convinced the reason that number is so low is due to lack of understanding on the adviser's part. Because so few advisers recommend these types of investments, it leaves the door wide open to those advisers who "get it." My goal with this book is to open your eyes to things you never thought possible.

How the Rich got Rich (Including Your Biggest Clients)

The Forbes list of the 400 wealthiest individuals in the United States provides an interesting basis for a discussion of private investments. In 2020, of the 400 individuals on the list, 98 of them inherited their money, one made his money in the public markets (although not in a traditional way), and 301 earned their wealth in private investments (30 of those in real estate). If we remove those individuals who inherited their wealth, we see that of the 302 remaining wealthiest people in the U.S., effectively 100% of them made their money in private investments. If you separate private companies and real estate, it breaks down to 90% private equity and 10% real estate.

You may be thinking to yourself right now, "Wait a second. Jeff Bezos made his money in Amazon and that is a publicly traded stock." You are correct. However, Amazon didn't start out as a public stock, so Jeff Bezos' wealth was ultimately derived from a private company.

Amazingly, 100% of the wealthiest people in this country made money through private investments, and less than 14% of advisers are even recommending these types of investments to their clients. How did your wealthiest clients make their money? I would bet that they are no different than the Forbes 400. If by some miracle, they made their money in the traditional public markets, then why do they need an adviser anyway?

Let's take a look at a common financial advice scenario . . .

Shirley has a client named Elizabeth who started a business from scratch 30 years ago and recently sold it for $10 million. Over those years, Elizabeth has also made investments, including real estate that she still owns, and they have done quite well for her. She takes her $10 million in sale proceeds to Shirley, an adviser, who promptly allocates her $10 million into a portfolio of stocks, bonds, exchange-traded funds (ETFs) and mutual funds.

Does this make any sense? The client knows private equity and real estate and has had significant success with both. Why not consider allocating some of the sale proceeds to private equity and real estate to round out Elizabeth's new portfolio?

Warren Buffet is famous for his advice to investors, "Never invest in a business you cannot understand."

In the example above, does the investor understand her new investments, the underlying businesses or the "why" behind the portfolio? It seems unlikely that she would. I remember sitting down with clients as an adviser and going to great lengths to explain to them the rationale for their asset allocations, the reason for the stock or manager selection, the correlation, alpha, beta and standard deviation. It always surprised me how quickly they forgot almost everything we discussed. These were very smart people that put an incredible amount of faith in their advisers. The good news is that there is a lot of room for advisers to engage their clients with their investments.

Give Your Clients What They Want

In order for advisers to have happy clients, their investments need to meet four main criteria. Their investments should:

1) be understandable to the investor
2) form a connection with the investor
3) be profitable for the investor
4) do good in the world

Private funds make it easy to meet all four requirements. They can give investors access to investments that are often easier to understand than the public markets, provide an ethical advantage that includes a great story and connection to the investment, and offer the opportunity to yield a nice return. Not only that, but private funds can be designed to create jobs, help further technological advancement, provide services to lower income market segments or help the environment, to name a few.

Imagine putting investment opportunities like these in front of your clients. What if your clients were excited to visit with you to see the updates on their portfolio—and by updates, I mean the stories not just the numbers? What if they could drive by or even touch and feel their investment? What if they were constantly peppering you with questions about the investment opportunity? What if they couldn't help bragging to their friends about how cutting-edge you are?

This type of client is engaged in a story and cannot wait to see how it ends. A client that is engaged like this will also be far more understanding and resilient if the markets turn south. It is ironic that most adviser's clients often understand the private markets better than the adviser. It isn't a knock on the adviser, it is just a reality that most wealthy clients have a lot of experience with real estate and private companies. Advisers, on the other hand, are almost solely focused on the public markets, and because we typically discount the things we don't understand, the cycle is perpetuated. Meanwhile, wealthy individuals may give advisers their public stock portfolios, but I can assure you they are going elsewhere for their more sophisticated investments like private equity and real estate.

Do your clients invest all their money with you? If the answer is no, they are going around you. Do your clients ever call you to liquidate some of their stocks so they can buy into something else? If so, you can be assured that the assets you are managing for them are not their priority, probably because there is less of a connection. This book will go a long way to explain how you can avoid being left out of the big money and become the center of your client's investing world.

Stop Ignoring Alternative Investments

In the investment advisory industry, we often refer to anything that isn't publicly traded like a listed stock or mutual fund as an "alternative" investment.

According to Siblisearch, the combined U.S. Stock Market (including NYSE, NASDAQ and OTCQX) total over $50 trillion in assets as of December 31, 2020. According to Prequin, the global private markets are $6.5 trillion. For the benefit of their clients, investment advisers should give private markets a serious look because, after all, almost every one of those public companies started out private. Private investments are often the seeds of the greatest brands and companies.

It's true that private investments are "alternative" to what advisers traditionally offer, but they are common investments to the wealthy. Advisers often say there are more unknowns about alternatives and that they are less liquid, but what they don't say (perhaps because they don't know) is that the biggest endowments, pensions and wealthiest individuals in the world use private funds as core allocations in their portfolios. Private funds (i.e., hedge funds, private equity funds, real estate funds) are definitely worth exploring for your accredited and qualified purchaser clients.

I am a former adviser, and I have since worked with many other advisers over the years. A common criticism of advisers in our industry is that they are lazy. I think a better description is "generic." Advisers spend a lot of time trying to differentiate themselves by their asset allocations or their fees, but to most clients it all looks the same.

Assets Under Management 2020: $6.5 Trillion

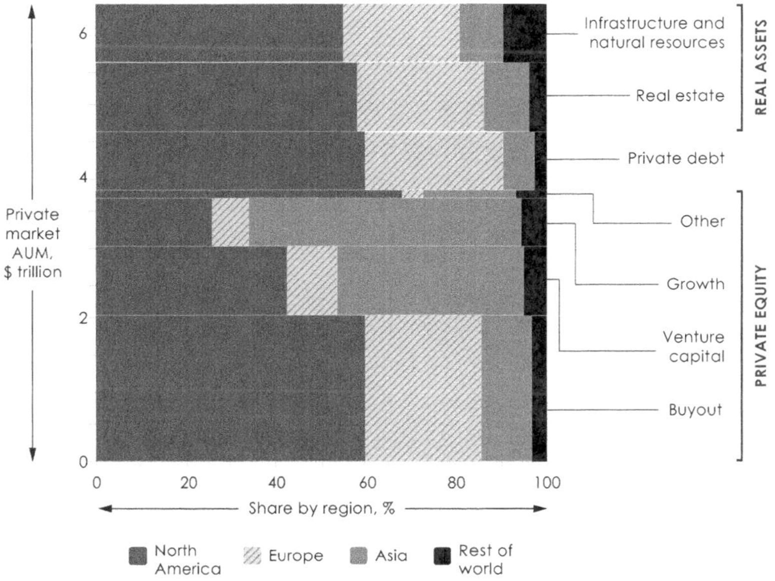

Source: Preqin

Creating an Advantage for Your Clients

Gaining an advantage in the marketplace is something that every adviser can do by simply opening up the universe of investment options to their clients. You will be far more likely to win bigger deals than advisers who are trying to differentiate themselves with only their mutual fund allocations and separate account strategies. You can be the adviser who offers both separate accounts AND private funds. Many stock market investments feel vanilla for the truly wealthy, and every adviser has some version of those strategies. There is nothing wrong with vanilla offerings, but when you are trying to land big clients, you will get lost in the crowd unless you throw in some chocolate, strawberry and maybe even some mint chip to get their attention!

Here is an example of how an adviser can position a private fund offering to increase their business exponentially:

We recently helped an adviser with a biotech venture capital fund that includes an individual who I will call Dominic. Dominic is very high profile and the head of one of the world's foremost medical institutions. He is part of the general partnership running the private fund and has his finger on the pulse of the new biotechnology. Dominic is the kind of guy you want to help run your biotech investments. He sees all the incubating technology, knows all the players and can get investors in on the ground floor of up-and-coming solutions. Talk about an unfair advantage for the investor! Not only that, but there is a team of other independent medical professionals who serve to advise the fund as they make their investments.

As an example, Dominic invested in Moderna at a very early stage and today, after developing a vaccine for Covid-19, Moderna is worth approximately $52 billion as of the publishing of this book. Imagine presenting a fund offering like this to your best accredited investor clients. How would they react? How would their image of you change? If you can show this type of offering to your clients, you have just created an edge. You will become memorable and more trusted. It doesn't even matter if they decide to invest or not. Your clients now see you differently. You are now a player in the investment industry, not just a spectator!

This biotech fund is a great example of the type of investment that investors really connect with. The good that a fund like this can do in treatment advances for cancer, alzheimer's, heart disease and other conditions make it easy for anyone to connect with the cause. It is also easy for investors to repeat the big names that they are investing alongside ("you would know them") and describe some of the anecdotal successes like Moderna. In fact, investors will usually take every opportunity they can get to boost their own social standing by describing their special investments. Don't be surprised when your client's friends call you to learn more about the offering. Client referrals will become a regular part of your business and they are far more valuable than paid advertising. And all of this happens because you created an "edge" for your clients. You gave them something they couldn't get anywhere else.

The Benefits of Limited Transparency

Public markets are considered fully transparent with every investor working off the same information. Advisers are striving for some sort of edge or differentiator for the accounts or asset pools they manage. Advisers who use mutual funds and actively manage ETFs often talk about manager selection as the key. The special managers can see things in the data that others miss, which gives them a unique advantage. The problem that mutual fund managers face is that their advantages don't last very long.

I have a friend, Matt Faulkner, who was the lead engineer for the Furniture Row Racing NASCAR team. Furniture Row Racing competed from 2005 to 2018 and was the only NASCAR team headquartered west of the Mississippi. They won the NASCAR championship in 2017. One day I met Matt for lunch and we were talking about his team's recent NASCAR championship. Matt was already preparing for the next season. It was fascinating to hear him describe the week-to-week process of preparing for a race. I have never forgotten what Matt said.

Matt told me that during the race, they are analyzing not only their own car, but all the other leading cars in the race to see what modifications other teams had made and evaluating whether or not they are working. He said that every week, they make modifications to their car to try to get the slightest edge by trying something new or copying a competitor from the previous week. It is literally a game of seconds. Matt shared that any advantage they have only lasts for a week because by the next week others have copied them.

Sound familiar? This is the equivalent of trading in the public markets. It is a rat race.

Private markets, by contrast, are less transparent and less liquid, which can be a really good thing—especially if you have an excellent manager like Dominic and his biotech venture fund example. The lack of transparency allows the manager to sustain an advantage for their investors longer, and all out of the sight of public competitors.

The Magic of Exclusivity

Researchers Worchel, Lee and Adewole performed an interesting study about cookies in 1975. In the study, they placed ten identical chocolate chip cookies in a cookie jar. Then they placed two, also identical cookies, in a separate cookie jar. The researchers then asked participants to place a value on the cookies. Interestingly, the participants valued the cookies in the nearly empty jar by almost twice as much. Why? It is the scarcity principle.

Imagine that you are visiting with a very wealthy prospect who is trying to decide whether or not to use your services. She is interviewing several other advisers. You discuss your advice approach and show her several investment strategies that you might recommend and can deploy in a separate account, just like every other adviser (the full cookie jar). Your offering is interesting, but seems similar to some of the other pitches she has already heard and leaves her unclear about which adviser to choose. Then you show her your latest private offering that is currently securing commitments to finance the new Four Seasons Hotel that will be built in town. It only has five spots left for $1 million each (two cookies in the jar). Now she's interested. She sees you differently. She didn't even know that she could be a part of something like that. After all, she loves staying at the Four Seasons. You show her pictures of the plans and some stats and returns on other Four Seasons hotels in other cities and she loves all of it. Not only that, but there is a deadline that she must meet or she will miss out.

Who just secured an investment in the private fund? Which adviser got the separate account business, too? Which adviser just took investment advice to a whole new level in the prospect's eyes? It won't even matter that it may cost more than other investments, that her money may be locked up for five years or that you get 20% of any profits—she is thrilled that you gave her an investment with a connection and an advantage. Not to mention it was exclusive. Don't be surprised when four of her friends call you to fill the last available spots? Now you are using the magic of exclusivity!

Does this seem crazy or too much? Whether you realize it or not, this is happening all day every day by savvy investment advisers all over the country. In fact, the example I shared about the Four Seasons Hotel is a real example. Advisers like the ones who put that fund together are eating your lunch. Do you want to join the big leagues of investment management? If so, keep reading.

The Illiquidity Premium

How often do you talk to your clients about investing for the long term? Most likely you show them charts and give them numbers showing investment cycles and average investment returns over time. You are likely making the point that markets go up and down and that it is important to not sell at the bottom or buy at the top. You also probably spend a lot of time helping your clients avoid panic when the markets drop.

Would you like to help your clients stay invested and make your life easier at the same time? Consider private funds as investments for your high-net-worth (HNW) clients. Private funds are generally not as liquid as mutual funds and stocks. They require investors to commit for a longer period of time that may range from months to years, and that is a good thing!

Mutual funds are an excellent public vehicle, but one of the biggest challenges that mutual fund managers face is managing the fund's liquidity. Mutual funds have people buying in and selling out every single day. This churn can create a real problem on performance.

If Warren Buffet was subject to the constraints of a mutual fund, his performance would likely never have been so impressive. Instead, he has been free to make investments and give them time to grow into the opportunities he envisioned. Private fund structures provide breathing room for advisers to find great opportunities for investors with the correct investor expectations. What could you do for a client's portfolio if you had a guaranteed five, seven or even ten years to grow their money?

Some advisers use private fund lock-up periods and illiquidity as an excuse not to recommend them. I would argue that for wealthy clients, it is a great reason to allocate a percentage of client assets to them. Everyone should be a long-term investor to some degree, especially accredited investors. Private funds are a great vehicle to help investors do the right thing for their clients and themselves.

Advisers who recommend that clients invest in private funds are solidifying long-term relationships with their clients and long-term fee income as well.

Key Points

1. A good investment adviser will add value to his or her clients by giving them something others cannot — an edge.
2. Private investments are, by definition, less transparent which provides investors an advantage over their competitors.
3. Private investments are exclusive, and everyone wants to be part of an exclusive club.
4. Private investments usually require longer holding periods, which is what advisers recommend to their clients anyway.

Exercise: Imagine you could offer your clients an investment like Dominic's. Make a list of current clients, friends, associates and acquaintances who would be interested.

2

You Are A Private Equity Investor

ENTREPRENEURSHIP IS THE LIFEBLOOD OF OUR ECONOMY AND every entrepreneur is a private equity investor. From the time that settlers moved west for land or gold to today's technology startup founders, it is the same spirit of innovation that drives it all.

Your RIA is a Private Company

We are frequently so caught up in our work that we rarely take a step back to see that our companies are our biggest investments, both in time and money. And because our companies are privately held, it logically follows that you and I are heavily invested in private equity.

I recently had a conversation with the CEO of a successful RIA firm that manages billions of dollars and when the conversation turned toward private equity, he said, "I just assume that all private equity deals are going to blow up."

It wasn't appropriate to say at the time, but I wanted to ask him, "Is that how you feel about your firm? Is your private equity venture (meaning his RIA) going to blow up for you and your investors?" Of course he would say "no" because he understands his business and he can clearly see the opportunity. The main reason why he and most advisers are nervous about alternative investments is because they don't understand them.

My First Private Equity Investment

Even when I was younger, I loved business. I used to hold carnivals in my backyard and charge admission when I was eight years old. When I was in middle school, I bought large bins of candies and sold them out of my backpack at school at a tremendous profit (even after accounting for the ones I gave away to teachers). Like many kids, I babysat and mowed lawns, but it wasn't until I discovered window washing that I really hit my stride.

My dad had a friend whose sons were heading off to college. My dad told me that they had earned enough money to pay for college by washing windows, and he suggested I talk to them. I set up a time and received a one-hour training on how to wash windows and I caught the vision immediately. I cleverly decided to call my business "Adam's Window Washing." Despite the generic name, I was very successful. At 16 years old, I was regularly making about $50 per hour, while my friends were making minimum wage at fast food restaurants. I was hooked. I knew I would be an entrepreneur for the rest of my life.

Alta Trust is Born

I graduated from Brigham Young University in December of 2001 with a degree in Global Trade. My plan was to work internationally, but those hopes were dashed when all hiring froze in the wake of the recent 9/11 terrorist attacks. Aside from a job offer as an assistant manager at Toys R Us, I had nothing.

My dad was a financial planner and in one of our conversations, he suggested that I work for him. I joined my dad right after graduation. He worked as both an investment adviser representative and a broker/dealer representative. Less than a year after I joined, my dad and I decided to go independent and we created our own RIA. My dad was generous with me and gave me a percentage of the company in return for a lower salary. I didn't want a handout, but I also didn't have any money so that worked just fine for me.

We grew our RIA, and added a recordkeeping and third-party administration company to it as well. After about eight years, we realized that in order to reach our goals, we needed a strong trust company as a partner. The trust companies we knew tended to be either too big or too antiquated in their thinking for all the things we wanted to accomplish, so we decided to start a trust company of our own.

It didn't take long for other RIAs to want to use our newfound trust powers to help grow their businesses. To make a long story short, we sold the RIA and recordkeeping companies and have been focused on helping other RIAs through Alta Trust ever since.

I was just beginning my career, and I was already in the thick of private equity. I loved it! I loved the idea of starting with nothing and turning it into something. I loved the ability I had to control my own destiny.

Your Private Equity Story

I know that my story isn't unique. You have your own path that you have followed to get where you are. It would be impossible for you to teach all the lessons that you have learned over the years, and that is my point with this book. You have more expertise than you probably think you do. Just like me, you have developed instincts, principles and criteria for making good investments based on your experiences. Because you have failed in the past, you can succeed in the future. You know what to do and what not to do to help investors grow their investments and secure their future. You don't have to teach them all you know, but you should use your expertise to do it for them.

Because you have a business, whether you realize it or not, you have a track record in private equity. You may have it in real estate, and you may also have a track record suitable for a hedge fund. But don't worry, even if you don't, I will show you how to develop or even borrow a track record.

Low Profile Private Equity

When we think of private equity, we tend to have visions of multi-billion-dollar mega deals and newspaper articles announcing the latest acquisitions. That may be the most high-profile kind of private equity, but it is not the only kind. You can create your own private equity structure on a smaller scale that is just as lucrative.

Not too long ago, I was asking a friend for business advice. The conversation turned to her upcoming business plans. She indicated that she was planning to start another company (in the same industry) in a different geographic region. When I asked her how long it would take her to get up and running and be profitable, she answered, "Immediately!" Because she had done this several times before, she had all the people in place, including clients, to get started.

I remember thinking, "That is the kind of investment that everyone wants." The risk is so low because of her experience and connections that the investment becomes a lay-up, if not a slam dunk.

I would bet you a steak dinner that you have more than one person in your network that could do exactly the same thing. Maybe you are that person. A future private equity deal might be right under your nose.

Key Points

1. Every entrepreneur is a private equity investor.

2. Americans generally love private equity.

3. Private equity doesn't have to be big. In fact, oftentimes it is small.

Exercise: In what areas do you have particular experience? Who do you know that could set up a company and be almost immediately successful? What kind of company would that be?

3

Types of Private Funds

THERE ARE THREE PRIMARY VERSIONS OF A PRIVATE FUND. THEY include hedge funds, private equity funds and real estate funds. Here we will address each one in detail.

Hedge Funds

Everyone is familiar with the term "hedge fund." It conjures up thoughts of Wall Street and high stakes trading. While that can be the case, there are many hedge fund versions. In fact, there are even hedge funds that don't "hedge."

According to the Hedge Fund Association, there are approximately 10,000 active hedge funds in the United States which constitute a $3.2 trillion industry. One common misconception about hedge funds is that they are very risky when, in reality, most hedge funds only use derivatives to provide downside protection, and many don't use derivatives at all. One of their upsides is that they typically weight most of the manager's compensation toward performance or success fees.

COMMON INVESTOR TYPES

SAMPLE PRIVATE FUND (HEDGE)

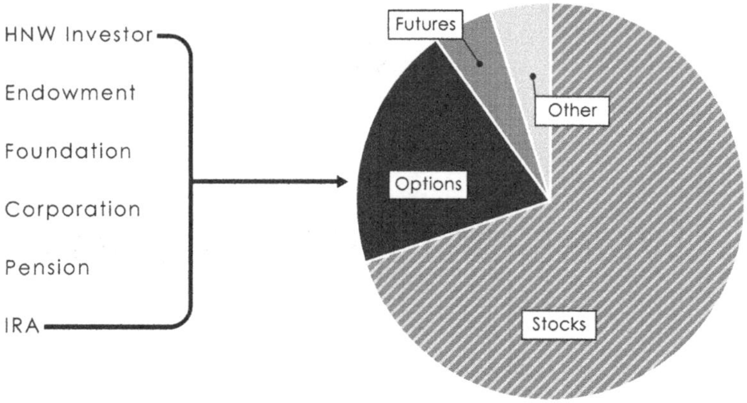

HEDGE FUND STRATEGY TYPES	
Strategy Type	**Description**
Aggressive Growth	Invests in equities and derivatives that are expected to experience acceleration in growth; the fund hedges by shorting equities. Tends to be long-biased.
Distressed Securities	Buys equity, debt or trade claims at deep discounts of companies in or facing bankruptcy or reorganization.
Emerging Markets	Invests in equity or debt of emerging (less mature) markets, derivatives and foreign currencies. Short selling is usually not available in emerging markets and, therefore, effective hedging is often not available.
Income	Invests with primary focus on yield or current income. May employ leverage to buy bonds and sometimes fixed income derivatives in order to profit from principal appreciation and interest income.

Strategy Type	Description
Macro	Aims to profit from changes in global economies and governments.
Market Neutral – Arbitrage	Attempts to hedge out most market risk by taking offsetting positions, often in different securities of the same issuer.
Market Neutral – Securities Hedging	Invests equally in long and short equity portfolios, generally in the same sectors of the market.
Market Timing	Invests across different asset classes depending on the manager's view of the economic or market outlook.
Opportunistic	Invests in themes that may vary widely as opportunities arise, such as IPOs and sudden price changes in companies.
Multi-Strategy	Invests across various strategies simultaneously to realize short- and long-term gains.
Short Selling	Sells securities short in anticipation of being able to rebuy them at a future date at a lower price.
Special Situations	Invests in event-driven situations such as mergers, hostile takeovers, reorganizations or leveraged buyouts.
Value	Invests in securities perceived to be selling at deep discounts to their intrinsic or potential worth.
Fund of Funds	Invests in one or more hedge funds, usually providing diversification across market sectors and managers.

Common Reasons for Launching a Hedge Fund

Almost all advisers offer their strategies through separately managed accounts (SMAs). It is common for trading to be automated across many client accounts and even across many custodians for those advisers who trade away. So why would an adviser go to the trouble and expense of creating a hedge fund?

▶ Allowing for Smaller Account Sizes

Consolidating smaller accounts into one large omnibus account is a great way to create scale and increase margins for an investment manager. In some cases, it also reduces trading costs and increases buying power—both great advantages to the investor. For example, we had an RIA ask us to consolidate many accounts that each had to be traded manually across several strategies into three funds.

In other instances, a manager can't access certain investments in smaller accounts due to hard minimums or the nature of the portfolio does not lend itself to smaller accounts. This is where a fund can help consolidate assets for easier operations, as well as provide investors with a full portfolio.

▶ Trading / Transparency

It is not uncommon for investors to place certain restrictions on a portfolio that requires special attention and reduces the trading efficiency for an adviser. Maybe a client doesn't want anyone to sell his Apple stock or maybe they like playing "Monday morning quarterback" on the investments you select. Having a private fund eliminates this issue because the adviser is trading a pool and the investor is a limited partner or a passive investor in the pool. In addition, the fund only needs to be as transparent as the adviser chooses, so investors can focus on returns and not critique specific investment decisions.

Stickier Assets

While it is true that hedge funds have become both increasingly less expensive and more liquid, they are still far stickier assets than mutual funds and exchange-traded funds and with good reason. Purchasing shares of a mutual fund or exchange-traded fund is as simple as a few clicks of a mouse. It is also just as easy to sell out mutual funds. Selling out of a hedge fund, by contrast, requires a notification and must meet different gates such as lock-up periods and notice periods prior to liquidation. This means that the mutual fund and ETF positions usually get liquidated first by an investor.

A New Strategy Launch

Hedge funds are a great way to launch a new strategy into the marketplace. They are flexible and affordable (at least the way we do it at Alta Trust). In some cases, advisers may launch two or three strategies and incubate them with sponsor money to gain a track record. At the end of six months or a year, they take the strategy or strategies that performed well out to the market.

Charging Performance Fees

It is not uncommon for investment advisers to use private funds as a vehicle to charge a performance allocation or take a carried interest on investment performance. These are common arrangements in private funds and it helps to not only facilitate and justify the conversation with clients, but it is also to their benefit from a tax standpoint. In fact, it should be malpractice for any adviser to charge a performance fee to a client account outside of a fund because it causes the client to pay unnecessary taxes.

Whatever your motivations, a hedge fund might make sense for you and your firm in order to manage client assets in the most efficient and cost-effective manner.

Hedge Fund Assets in Billions

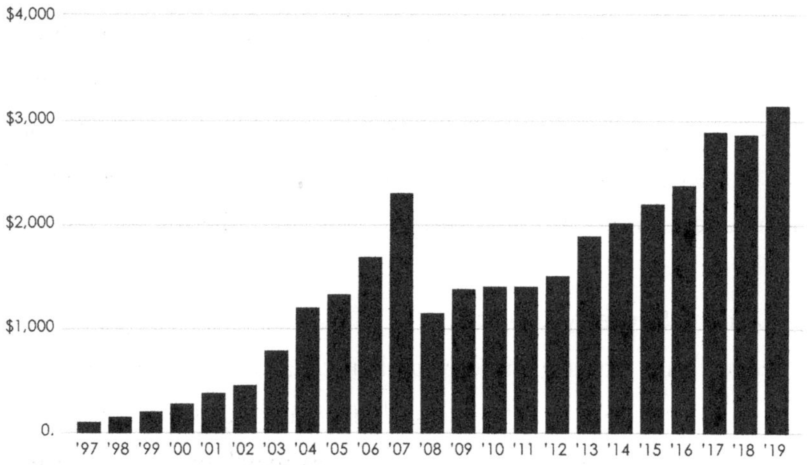

Source: BarclayHedge

Private Equity Funds

We hear about private equity in the news all the time. While most people generally know what it is, many advisers only look at it superficially without realizing how they can use private equity for their clients. When you hear the words "private equity," you likely think of corporate raiders buying up companies, picking them apart for profits and leaving the remains in a heap in their wake.

While this does happen from time to time, it is not usually how private equity works. This chapter will be an eye-opener to most advisers who take the time to really understand private equity. A private equity fund might not be out of the realm of possibilities for the right adviser.

A private equity fund or "PE" fund invests long-term capital in private (or at times, public) companies in return for an equity stake in one or more companies. The equity stake is generally not available to be freely traded on a public exchange.

Private equity funds are generally established as closed-end funds, meaning the funds have a finite lifespan (e.g., seven years). They also tend to operate as "blind pools," which means that each fund has a clearly defined target investment (e.g., late-stage U.S. biotech) but investors do not know, nor will they have a say in, the portfolio companies chosen by the general partner.

Let's start our discussion of PE funds by looking at the different parties and their roles.

General Partner / Sponsor

The general partner or sponsor, which may be your RIA if you choose, is completely responsible for managing the fund and is a fiduciary to the limited partners. The general partner must manage the private equity fund in the best interests of the investors. In some private equity structures, the general partner is owned by a private equity firm, providing additional separation and limitation of liability. The general partner issues capital calls to investors and manages all investment and divestment decisions in accordance with the private equity fund mandate set forth in the fund offering documents.

Frequently, the general partner will commit capital to the fund so they can have some "skin in the game." This generally ranges from 1% to 5% of committed capital. In some cases, the general partner will receive a "deemed contribution," which basically means that an investor contributes their capital for them in exchange for a lower fee.

Limited Partners (Investors)

Limited partners or "LPs" are the investors or shareholders in the private equity fund. The LPs contribute the capital and are considered passive investors with no say in the day-to-day management of the fund or in any of the investment decisions. In turn, the LPs are only liable to the extent of their investment in the private equity fund. Investors can include high-net-worth individuals, foundations, endowments, insurance companies, banks, trusts, public and private pensions, family offices and other funds. Investors make capital commitments upon subscribing to the fund. Capital commitments, just as they sound, are financial commitments to the fund, which will be requested or "called" at a later date by the general partner. The general partner is then able to draw down the capital it needs when it is ready to make investments.

Investment Manager (Sub-Adviser)

The general partner may delegate some of their duties to an investment manager. Usually this will include the day-to-day management of the fund, sourcing and evaluating potential portfolio companies, managing the fund's audit and reporting, as well as investor communications. The investment manager is paid a fee for providing these services, which is typically a portion of the general partner's fees.

Portfolio Companies

A standard private equity fund will typically invest in 10 to 15 companies over its life; these are called "portfolio companies." Prior to the companies being invested in, they are referred to as "target" companies. The fund is usually restricted from investing more than a certain percentage of the fund assets into any one portfolio company.

PE Fund Structure

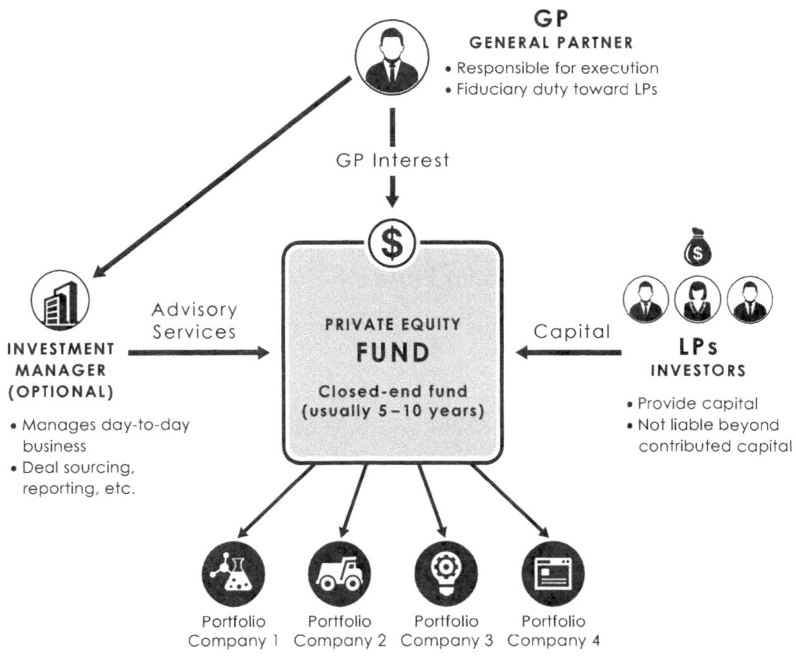

The Stages of a Private Equity Fund

▶ Fundraising (Offering Period)

A private equity firm raises capital for the fund by securing capital commitments from LPs. A private equity fund will typically have a target fund size, sometimes with a maximum capital threshold. Once the GP has secured enough in capital commitments, it will make its first capital call and initiate its "first close." The fund's first close commences when the general partner subscribes the investors into the fund. The due date of the capital call is the date of the first close. Usually the first close proceeds pay for fund expenses and make one or more initial investments. If a fund has its first close in the year 2021, then it is considered a "vintage 2021 fund." After the initial close, the general partner traditionally has 12 to 18 months to continue to secure additional capital commitments for the fund. The total amount raised by the private equity fund is called "committed capital."

▶ Investment / Drawdown Period

The length of the investment period varies, but it is typically about four to five years from the date of the first close. During that time, the general partner will make capital calls from time to time to deploy the committed or uncalled capital into new portfolio companies. Investors are usually given ten business days to fund a capital call. If an investor does not meet the capital call deadlines, then it will usually result in a penalty such as the general partner's right to charge high interest rates on late payments, the right to force the investor to sell their stake on a secondary market (likely at a significant discount), a limitation on the investor's interest in future profits, or possibly even charging any resulting losses to the investor's capital account. When an investor has met a capital call, it is referred to as "invested capital." A fund's committed but un-called capital is referred to in the industry as "dry powder."

Exit / Divestment Period

The private equity fund offering documents will typically provide for a five- to ten-year period that includes fundraising, investing, holding and exiting. A common provision in these types of funds is to allow the general partner to exercise two successive one-year options to extend the term of the fund if necessary. Exits typically come in the form of an acquisition or an initial public offering (IPO) or secondary sale (to another PE firm).

Lifecycle of a PE Fund

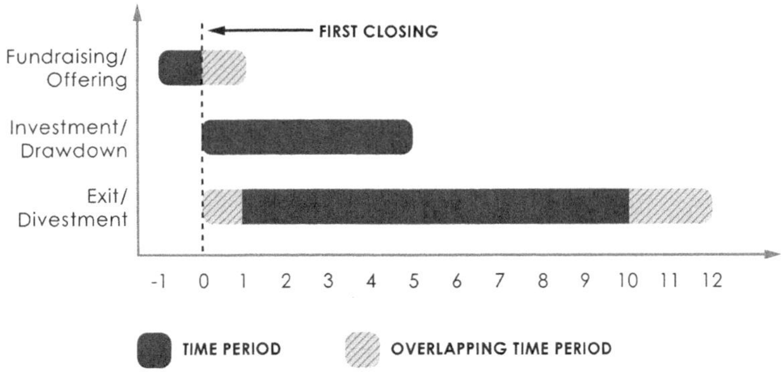

▶ The Next Fund

It isn't hard to imagine that raising capital for the second and third PE funds will be much easier once the private equity firm has a successful first fund. Generally, after a current fund has deployed 75% of its capital or met some other milestone outlined in the fund offering documents, the general partner can begin fundraising for its next fund. General partners are particularly interested in trying to secure reinvestments by investors who just experienced a successful exit from a fund.

▶ The J Curve

One important consideration for both general partners and investors to understand about a PE fund is that they may lose money or break even during the first few years as fees are being paid and investments are being sourced. The tendency to lose money at the beginning is depicted as the "J Curve."

J Curve simply refers to the tendency of PE funds to have negative returns in the early years, while the fund shoulders many upfront expenses and the general partner has not had time to put all the money to work. Assuming the fund portfolio of companies matures in a positive way, the fund's value increases and overcomes the early negative performance. This can make it difficult to reflect accurate performance of the fund from year to year. The most accurate way to assess the performance of a private equity fund is after it is closed. The most common way to evaluate a private fund against its peers is with a private market equivalent or "PME." A PME is essentially a benchmark for private investments. PE fund performance and PMEs are calculated based on cash flows using an internal rate of return (IRR) calculation.

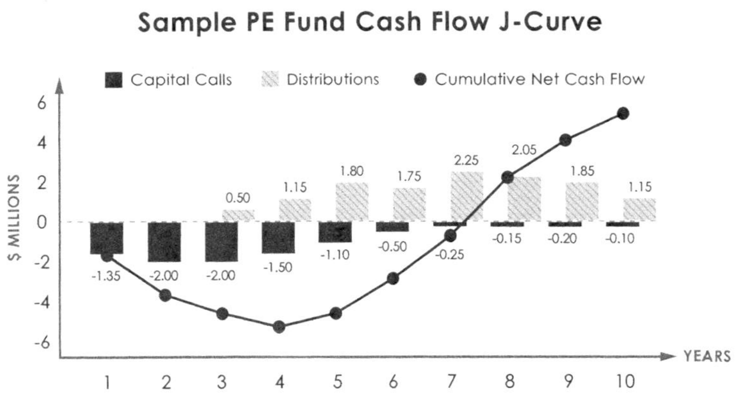

There are many different approaches to private equity. I have provided a summary of the primary investment strategies here.

PRIVATE EQUITY STRATEGIES	
Strategy Type	**Description**
Growth Equity	Invests in mature companies with proven businesses. The investments tend to be minority stakes and made with an eye toward using the capital and the PE firm's strengths to take the portfolio company to the next level.
Buyout/Leveraged Buyout	A controlling stake in the portfolio company so that the general partner can restructure the firm, including adding debt to the company's balance sheet, changing the management team, etc. This is the traditional approach to private equity.

Strategy Type	Description
The Diversified Fund	Has a broad mandate across geographies, industries and company sizes.
Mezzanine Fund	Invests in companies to provide them with capital for acquisitions, growth, recapitalization, etc. It is referred to as mezzanine because it fits between a pure equity or debt investment. Mezzanine investments usually take the form of preferred stock or unsecured, subordinated debt that can later convert to equity.
Restructuring/ Turnaround	Buys distressed companies to purchase at a deep discount with the aim of rehabilitating them and eventually selling them off.
Secondary Markets	Provides liquidity for limited partners of PE funds by purchasing their interests. The seller must sell at a deep discount.
Oil and Gas	Investments may take many forms such as operating interests, non-operating interests, mineral rights, pipelines, drilling and exploration, and master limited partnerships.
Infrastructure	Invests in public infrastructure projects such as airports, railroads, toll roads and utilities. They are generally considered a consistent source of non-debt income.
Private Investment in a Public Equity (PIPE)	This is a direct investment in a company already public, through a private placement. The investment is generally priced below the current market value of the company, giving the investors an immediate return while diluting the existing shareholders.
Private Debt	Versions of private debt strategies include general lending, direct lending, distressed debt, bridge financing, real estate debt, infrastructure debt, venture debt, etc.

Strategy Type	Description
Real Assets and Natural Resources	Investments may include precious metals, rare metals, mining, timber and agricultural investments.
Fund of Funds	Invests in one or more private equity funds, usually providing diversification across market sectors and managers.

Venture Capital Funds

A standard private equity fund seeks investments in mature, profitable companies that have room for market expansion. However, there is another form of private equity that focuses on startup companies referred to as venture capital or "VC" funds. VC funds are typically looking to make smaller investments in the early stages of a company. Oftentimes, the venture capital fund takes only a minority interest in early-stage companies and is betting on their future growth. In many cases, these companies are pre-revenue. Many household names, such as Peloton and Airbnb, are venture capital-backed companies.

Even though venture capital funds typically don't take a controlling stake in a company, investors may secure a seat on the company's board, and are usually very active in using their network and experience to help grow their portfolio companies. Venture capital funds may choose to focus their investments in certain industries and markets, as well as in different stages of the company such as: early stage, mid-stage or late stage. Those stages usually correlate to the various funding rounds: Seed, Series A, Series B, Series C.

VC FUNDING ROUND DESCRIPTIONS				
Funding Round	**Seed**	**Series A**	**Series B**	**Series C**
Stage	Proof of Concept	Revenue Growth	Growth	Scale
Areas of Focus	Product/ Service Development	Hiring, Operations, Marketing/ Branding	Hiring, Market Expansion	Acquisitions, New Markets
Typical Investment Amount	$0 – $1 million	$10 million	$15 – $25 million	$50 million

Number of venture capital deals in the U.S.
1995 – 2019

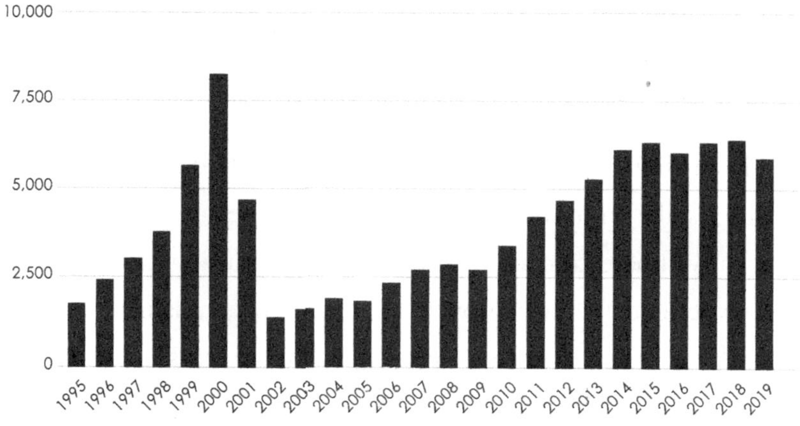

Source: PwC; CB Insights

Venture capital fundraising in the U.S.
2004 – 2019

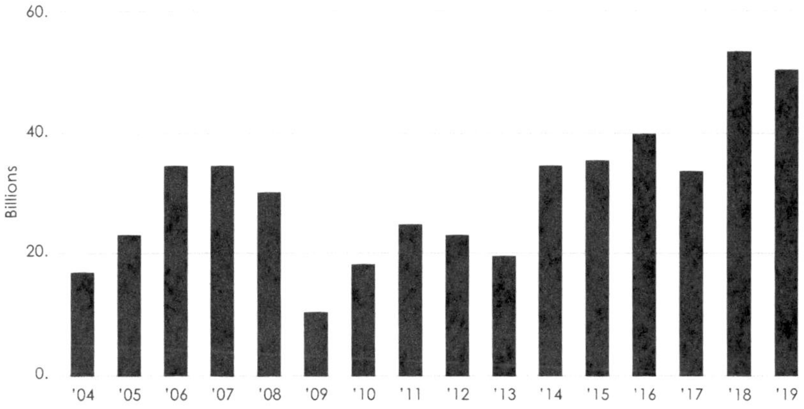

Source: Thomson Reuters; NVCA

Regardless of the details, VC investing is a high risk/high return game with general partners typically betting that one or two of their portfolio companies will go big and make up for the losses from the rest of their portfolio companies. Some examples of successful companies that were backed by venture capital money are Airbnb, DoorDash, SpaceX and Peloton.

One more interesting piece of information on venture funds is that they have been given a special accommodation by the government within 3c1 of the Investment Company Act of 1940 ('40 Act). A venture fund can have up to 250 accredited investors (as opposed to 100), as long as it doesn't raise over $10 million.

Number of Private Equity Funds by Type

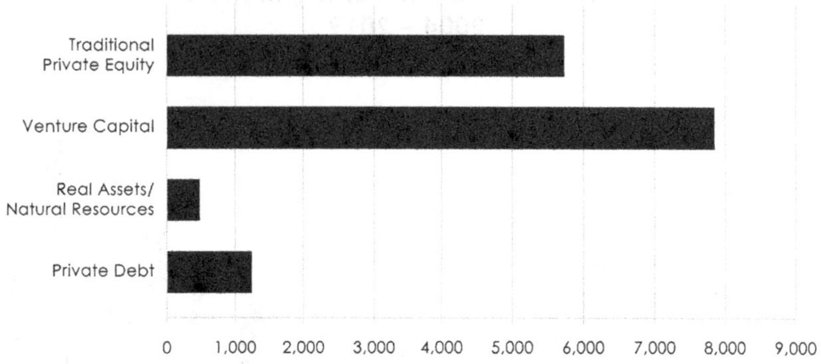

Source: Pitchbook as of 9/30/2020

I referenced some big names and successes in private equity funds, but the reality is that advisers just like you are launching PE funds every day as they build their personal brands. You don't have to be the biggest name to make a significant impact for your clients and yourself.

Real Estate Funds

Real estate funds usually follow the same structure as equity funds, but the real estate market is so large and prolific that the types of real estate funds vary widely. Real estate has been a reliable generator of wealth over the years and is a place where many investors, both public and private, have invested a lot of money. There are many ways to use real estate as an investment. Your clients may be looking for income, capital appreciation or even something speculative. Real estate funds are generally structured in a limited partnership or business trust, but they run the spectrum when it comes to liquidity.

We will discuss a few of the most common real estate investment strategies used in a private fund here.

REAL ESTATE INVESTMENT STRATEGIES	
Strategy Type	**Description**
Commercial	Invests only in commercial real estate.
Residential	Invests only in residential real estate.
Core	Buys and holds high-quality real estate.
Core Plus	Buys and holds real estate that may have more risk, but also more opportunity.
Value Add	Invests in real estate that may need major renovations or has low occupancy rates.
Opportunistic	Invests in turnaround projects and/or new developments.
Lending	Makes short-term loans collateralized by real estate. Loans usually include upfront fees (points) and high interest rates.
Opportunity Zones	Invests at least 90% of its assets in qualified opportunity zone investments. Can allow investors to defer gains from qualifying investments through 2026; investors can also defer gains for up to ten years.
Geography-Based	Invests in certain geographical areas only.
Agricultural	Invests in farm or ranch properties.
Fund of Funds	Invests in one or more real estate funds, usually providing diversification across market sectors and managers.

REITs

Real estate investment trusts (REITs) are commonly used by advisers, but have you ever considered creating your own?

There are three main types: equity, mortgage and hybrid REITs. A fund can qualify to be a REIT (and in our case, a private REIT) when it:

- Invests at least 75% of total assets in real estate, cash or U.S. Treasuries
- Derives at least 75% of gross income from rents, interest on mortgages that finance real property, or real estate sales
- Derives at least 95% of its gross income from such real estate sources and dividends or interest from any source
- Pays a minimum of 90% of taxable income in the form of shareholder dividends each year
- Is an entity that's taxable as a corporation, but usually pays little to no taxes
- Is managed by a board of directors or trustees
- Has at least 100 shareholders after its first year of existence
- Has no more than 50% of its shares held by five or fewer individuals during the last half of the taxable year
- Has shares that are fully transferable
- Has no more than 25% of its assets consisting of non-qualifying securities or stock in taxable REIT subsidiaries

In return for following these guidelines, the REIT mostly avoids the corporate double taxation. Instead, investors receive a 1099-DIV form at the end of each year.

Additional Real Estate Considerations

Holding the real estate directly in a fund creates a few other complexities. The fund will likely need to purchase insurance on the property, possibly hire a property manager, pay taxes, pay for maintenance, etc. All of this creates a great deal of complex accounting work, but the trade-off may be worth it as opposed to incurring the costs of investing in another fund.

Another consideration is the asset valuation. You need to have a strong methodology built around how the fund assets are to be valued. You can use annual appraisals, a cash flow model, comparable properties, a third-party valuation firm, etc. The method that you choose will be outlined in detail in the offering documents.

Finally, when you invest directly into properties, you have the option of borrowing to finance the acquisitions so that the capital you raise goes further. This can be a very powerful approach to magnifying returns, but it also creates additional risks and complexity, not to mention that the financing costs can be a drag on returns. If you do choose to leverage your portfolio, be aware that it can create unrelated business taxable income (UBTI) for your tax-exempt investors.

It's important to understand the differences of these three core structures, so that you don't waste time going down the wrong path.

GENERAL PRIVATE FUND CHARACTERISTICS BY FUND TYPE			
	Private Equity	**Hedge**	**Real Estate**
Open/Closed	Closed	Open	Either
Investment Funding	Capital Calls/ Drawdowns	Immediate	Either
Lock-Up Period	5 – 10 years	3 months – 1 year	Either
Incentive Fees	Yes	Yes	Yes

Key Points

1. Your investment strategy and target investors will determine your structure.
2. Hedge funds typically invest in more liquid securities and are usually open-end, continuous offerings.
3. Private equity funds typically invest in mature companies and are usually closed-end finite offerings that follow different stages in a lifecycle.
4. Venture capital is a type of private equity that invests in startup companies and usually takes a minority interest.
5. Real estate is usually structured more like private equity, but may have some hedge fund characteristics (e.g., continuously offered).

Exercise: Which of the three main types of private funds are you most prepared to launch right now? What investment strategy would you employ? Would you need a partner to help or do you have the necessary expertise? What type of fund would your clients love?

4

Private Fund Structures

NOW THAT WE HAVE LEARNED ABOUT THE THREE MAIN TYPES of private funds, it is time to dive into more detail about the specific types of structures we can use when launching a fund.

Special Purpose Vehicles

Special purpose vehicles or "SPVs" work great for single private equity investments and real estate deals. Often called "A Fund of One," this could look like a fund that invests in only one company or in a single apartment building. They also don't tend to have many investors, usually a handful of ten or so. An SPV is a simplified version of a full-fledged private fund.

Some of the benefits of an SPV include its simplicity to establish and manage; rolling up of investors into one entity for easier administration; and consolidation of control by the fund's general partner who is authorized to act on behalf of the pool, and in some cases acting as a buffer.

For advisers who are looking for them, there are one-off investment opportunities everywhere you look. It could be starting a new company, investing in one of your client's companies (be sure to disclose any conflicts of interest), financing a local government project, or a new piece of land that becomes available. When you just have one investment in a fund, the special purpose vehicle is easy, quick and inexpensive to set up. Don't be surprised if you begin seeing opportunities for SPVs everywhere.

Open-End vs. Closed-End

One important consideration for a private fund is whether the fund will be open-ended (continuously offered) or closed (does not accept new investors after a trigger event or a period of time). It is important to match up the maturities of your underlying investments with your fund provisions. Strategies that fit best in an open-end fund are those that allow you to easily put money to work so it doesn't create a performance drag on the portfolio. Hedge funds tend to be open-ended, private equity funds are usually closed, and real estate funds can go either way.

Fund of Funds

A fund of funds model is a simple way for most advisers to start. Using this model is very similar to creating an asset allocation model across mutual funds and ETFs. Assuming your fund is created, all you need to do is screen for the different fund types and create your allocations.

Screening funds can be a bit of a moving target. Private equity funds are opening and closing all the time, so timing is important. Depending on the target size of the target fund and the size of your fund, you may be able to negotiate better terms for your clients and yourself, or help your clients participate in a fund with a high minimum they could not access on their own.

One approach is to create a broadly diversified fund that includes several different types of funds with different managers. In real estate, this might look like a fund that owns other funds with focuses on a variety of areas such as commercial, residential or deeds of trust — or maybe even an infrastructure fund that owns assets like toll roads, airports, etc.

Another fund of funds approach would be to create your fund for a specific type of investment such as commercial real estate, and then achieve manager diversification by picking a handful of different funds.

Yet another approach may work if your goal is to get your investors access to a specific fund that may be somewhat exclusive with high minimums. This approach may lend itself to a special purpose vehicle that would be created for the sole purpose of investing in a target fund.

There are many high-quality hedge, private equity and real estate funds coming available regularly. A fund of funds approach can give investors a nice investment with manager diversification. It can also make day-to-day life a bit easier for the sponsor. A sponsor may use services like Prequin or Pitchbook to filter for the fund types they are looking for and to perform due diligence on the funds and managers, similar to what you may be doing in Morningstar for mutual funds.

Whatever your fund of funds approach may be, you will need to make sure to match your fund's terms and provisions with the underlying funds you use (e.g., redemptions, valuations, etc.). You will also need to be conscious of the total fees. Layering your fee on top of the fee for the underlying fund(s) can add up, but should be considered in the context of doing all of the fund work in-house, which can also be expensive.

The best part of the fund of funds approach is that it is fairly quick to launch, and you are able to lean on the expertise, reputations and credibility of the managers that you use. A fund of funds approach can make a lot of sense for an adviser's first fund.

Hybrid

A hybrid approach between the fund of funds and direct investing models makes sense when an adviser has an expertise in a specific area, but wants to round out the fund offering with other areas of expertise. Essentially, this means that a sponsor may invest a percentage of a fund's assets directly and the rest of the assets in other funds to round out a portfolio. We have even seen some sponsors who take this approach charge differently for direct investments versus fund investments.

Incubator Funds

An incubator fund provides a way to create a fund on a smaller scale and at a lower cost to prove a concept or provide a track record with sponsor money, hoping it can be turned into a full-scale fund in the future. While these are more common with hedge funds, they can work for open-ended real estate funds too.

Friends and Family Fund

This kind of fund is a small-scale fund that is only made available to a close-knit group of friends and family. The fund generally has very few investors and no management fees, making it simpler to administer and therefore less expensive.

Private Label Funds

Most advisers don't realize that they can engage brand name sub-advisers with good track records and good reputations they can lean on. They can brand the fund after either themselves or the sub-adviser (as agreed to by the sub-adviser) and they can highlight the expertise and pedigree of the adviser, effectively adopting the strategy as their own. This is a great approach for advisers looking to "borrow" a track record because they don't have their own yet.

Master / Feeder Structures

There are more master/feeder variations than you could possibly count, and even more reasons why you might want to use them. One of the most common is to block taxes for tax-exempt U.S. entities (UBIT) or possibly to block U.S. taxes for foreign investors. If these are your target investors, you should consider an offshore master/feeder structure. U.S. pension plans or other tax-exempt entities invest in the offshore fund (feeder), which then invests in the U.S. onshore fund (master) which holds the fund investments. The feeder fund only holds interests of the master fund. The offshore fund blocks any U.S. tax liabilities to its investors.

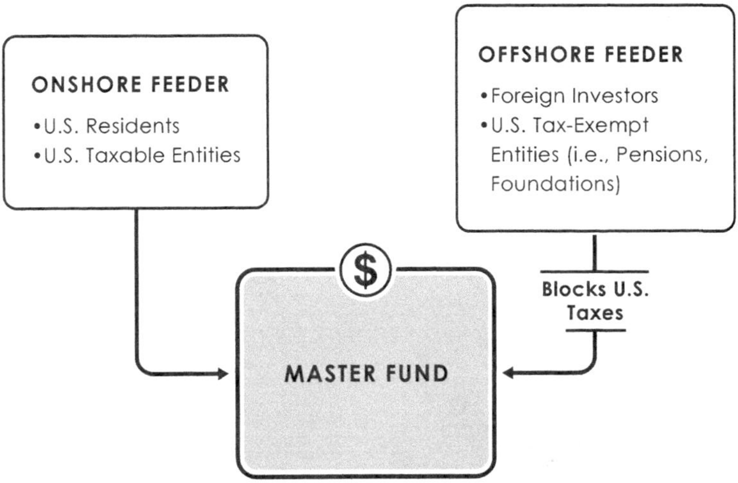

Parallel Funds

Parallel Funds can come in several forms, but a common scenario is a 3c1 and a 3c7 fund. The 3c1 fund can take up to 100 accredited investors and the 3c7 fund can facilitate up to 2,000 qualified purchasers before having to register with the SEC. They can both implement the same strategy and have the same holdings and operate side by side without the worry of fund integration, which we will discuss in detail later.

Another potential parallel fund situation can arise when an adviser sponsors two funds, one being specific to taxable investors and the other being specific to tax-exempt investors. This can allow for two private funds with the same strategy (except for the tax management) and likely not violate the integration rules.

Additionally, some managers may elect to spin off a parallel SPV that invests alongside a master fund, but only in a specific investment. This approach allows investors to gain additional exposure to a specific investment.

Parallel SPV Approach

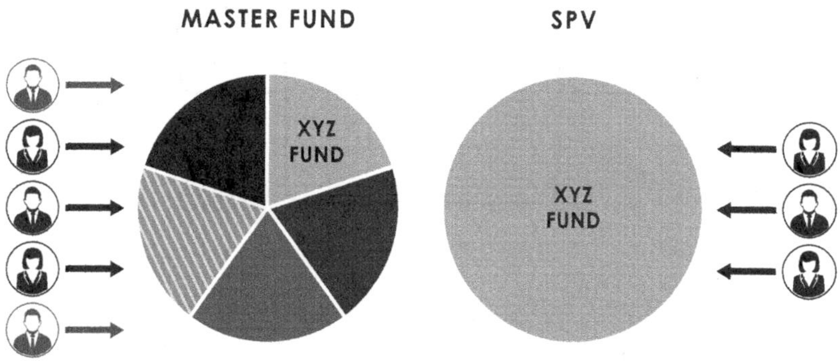

Blockers

Blocker entities are an advanced way to prevent tax liabilities to the fund and its investors. They usually come in the form of U.S.-based subsidiary entities (corporations and partnerships) or, as in the earlier example, an offshore fund.

SBIC Funds

Small business investment companies (SBICs) are part of a little-known program offered by the Small Business Administration (SBA). On March 12, 2018, the SEC adopted a final rule classifying SBICs as venture capital funds in response to the 2015 FAST Act. This means that SBICs qualify for the venture capital exemption mentioned earlier AND any SBIC assets will not count toward an exempt reporting adviser's $150 million registration requirement.

The SBIC program is a multi-billion-dollar investment program founded in 1958. Fund managers must go through a rigorous application process, but once they are approved they are eligible to borrow $2 for every $1 in capital they raise up to $175 million. Once the fund matures, the loan is paid back to the SBIC and the investors receive the remainder of the fund assets.

There are several investment limitations within the SBIC program, not the least of which is that the fund must invest in small businesses. For more information on the SBIC program, visit **www.sba.gov/inv**.

The SBIC Public-Private Partnership

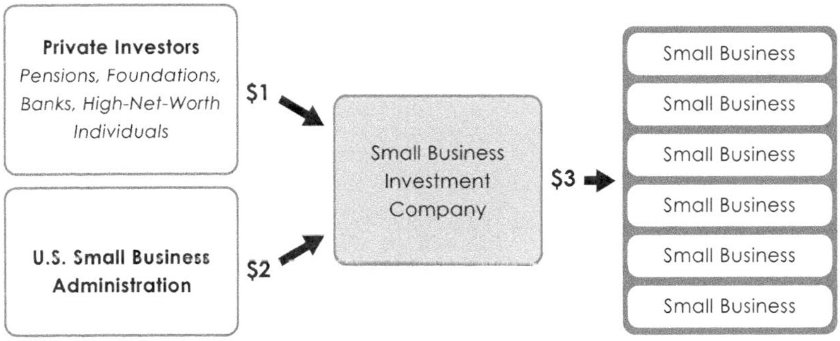

As mentioned earlier, except for those who inherited their money, all the Fortune 400 made their money in real estate and private investments. There are so many variations of ways to structure a private fund offering that it is very likely you will find a solution to the need you are trying to fill. You just need the right people to guide you along.

Key Points

1. Special purpose vehicles are extremely powerful funds if you know how to use them right.
2. A private fund of funds is the most familiar structure for most investment advisers.
3. There are many paths to success when launching and running a private fund.

5

Private Fund Strategies

HOPEFULLY BY NOW YOU ARE BEGINNING TO UNDERSTAND THE benefits of private investments. Advisers can always recommend that their clients invest directly into a third-party private offering. There are several alternative investment platforms built to facilitate those direct investments for adviser clients and that can be a great approach to using private funds. This book is not intended to address advisers recommending investments into a third-party private fund. Instead, the purpose of this book is to help investment advisers create and manage their own private funds. I hope that by now the beginnings of a private fund are starting to form in your mind.

What does it mean to create your own private fund? It means that you are creating your own hedge fund, real estate fund or private equity fund which can feel exciting and daunting all at the same time. It is true that creating and managing a fund is serious business and can't be done halfway. If you are going to do it, it needs to be done right with every "i" dotted and "t" crossed. These next chapters will help guide you through the process and keep you from making the mistakes that most rookies often make. I will explain the process clearly so that the idea of launching a fund becomes less daunting and more exciting.

There are so many reasons to create private funds that I can't name them all here. However, some of the common reasons include having more discretion over investments, trading and operational efficiencies, increasing a firm's brand, and having a structured offering or product. Other reasons include being able to offer clients something unique, offering greater diversification for clients, helping a community, taking advantage of specific opportunities, and so on.

I created my first private fund when I was 30 years old with my father and another partner. We did it at the request of several of our advisory clients who were clamoring for something different than the stock market. We considered several different investment options, but ultimately landed on an oil and gas deal. Our clients, who became investors, were thrilled to have something new and different to invest in. They felt like they were part of something bigger, something real. Our second private fund came just a year later and was created because of all the opportunities we uncovered from the first fund. The process was enlightening and fun, even despite all of the mistakes we made.

The thing that surprises advisers most about the private fund world is the sheer number of options available. Private funds are a place where advisers can exercise some freedom in an otherwise highly regulated industry. As you continue to read, I will navigate you through many options and variables and I will offer my opinion where it makes sense. But remember, just because you can do something doesn't mean you should. I want you to end up with a fund that is done right, is enjoyable and rewarding to you and is profitable for everyone involved. My goal is to help make the complex simple and to help you get your fund to market quickly and in the right way. I'll start by providing some different approaches advisers may take when creating private funds.

Private Fund Use Cases

Private funds are flexible vehicles, which means there are many ways to use them. I can't possibly imagine all the ways, but I will give you a common list of uses here.

Private Funds for Small Accounts

This approach is a classic. It can be tough to manage many different separate accounts. In some cases, advisers pass on accounts because they don't meet their minimum asset size. I have seen minimum asset sizes for a separate account from $50,000 to $500 million, so a small account is relative. I like to show advisers that they don't have to pass up "small" accounts if they have a private fund.

Example:

Recently, an RIA approached us to create a private fund because they were passing up too many "small" accounts. They had a minimum account size of $25 million. As it happened, their sales team encountered a lot of $5 and $10 million accounts that wanted their services, but it didn't make sense for them to manage accounts that size. A private fund allowed them to agree to those smaller clients and manage them all in one account efficiently. The private fund was slightly more expensive than a separate account, but for their smaller accounts it was better than not having their investment management at all!

This approach saves so much time and effort, even for large accounts. How much work does it take to create 100 separate accounts? How much work does it take to maintain each of those accounts? You're right, one fund with 100 investors seems like a winner!

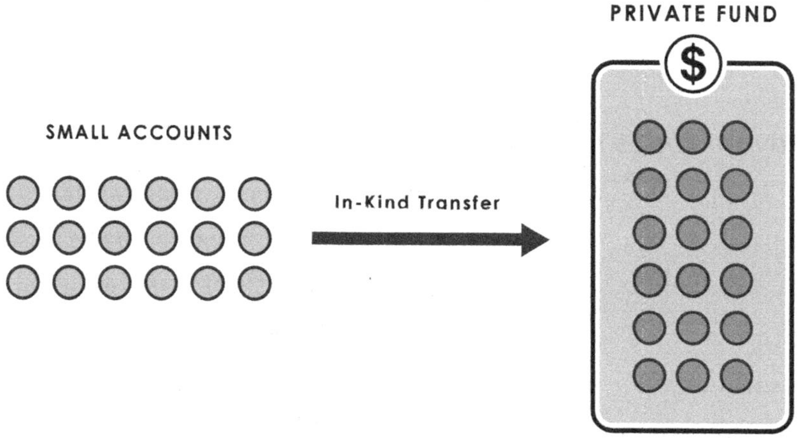

The Private Real Estate Approach

A few years ago, a forward-thinking adviser, Jeff, told me about an opportunity he had in town to buy some land and develop an apartment complex. He said he could easily raise the money from his client base, but had no idea how to even approach a project of this size. Jeff didn't have the expertise and was unsure where to start. I suggested he consider launching a private real estate fund. The structure of a fund like this makes it easy. The general partner can buy the land in the fund and hire the engineers and contractors to get the job done. Jeff didn't need to be an expert in real estate, he could hire expertise. He simply needed to be the visionary and put the right parties together.

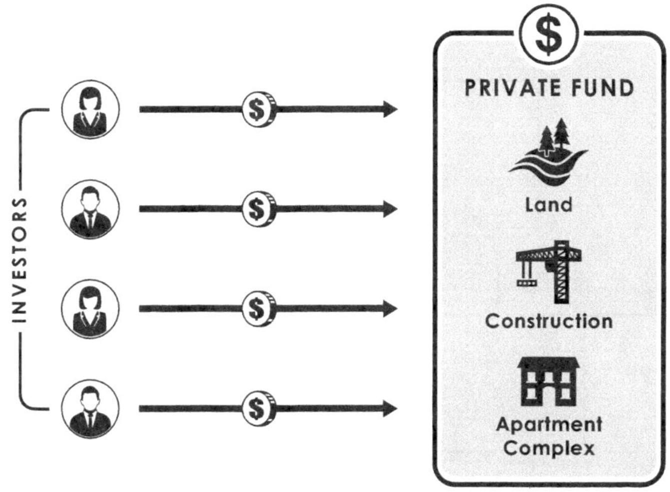

The Allocator Fund (Fund of Funds)

Don't have your own investment strategy? As discussed earlier, you can create a fund that invests in other funds. Just like a mutual fund allocation, you can create a unique fund of funds. It's easy to achieve great diversification for your clients and allow them to meet otherwise unattainable fund minimums by pooling their money in a fund.

Example:

One of our non-private fund clients recently lamented the fact that they didn't have anything beyond their separate account portfolios to offer two clients who each had separately sold their businesses, each for nearly $100 million. It didn't matter how good their separate accounts were, with that kind of money, they wanted something more. A private fund would have helped them satisfy their clients.

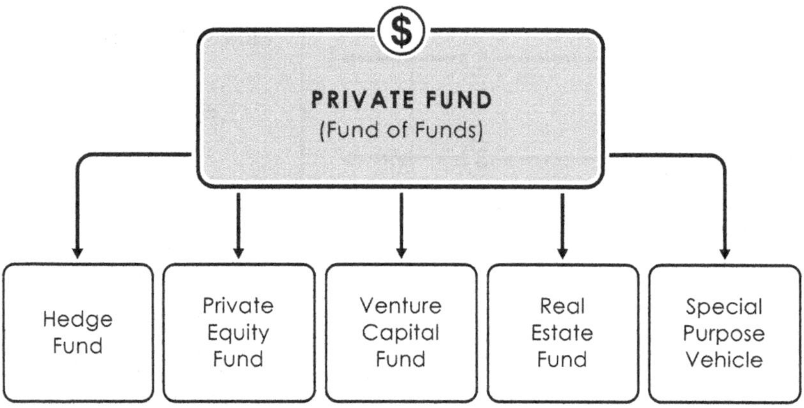

The Special Purpose Vehicle

We have discussed SPVs already, but I cannot overstate what a powerful tool they can be, despite their simplicity. This type of fund uses the same Reg D private offering exemption and is subject to all the same rules; however, it is built for a single purpose. The fund will only make a single investment. An SPV fund makes a lot of sense for pooling together investors who want to put $5 million or more into a single investment offering.

Example:

I have an adviser friend, Matthew, who came across a unique opportunity to invest in a CBD company that produces lotions and oils that provide a variety of medical benefits. They were looking for capital and Matthew saw it as a great opportunity for some of his clients. The terms that he negotiated were favorable, so he started a fund for the sole purpose of making this one investment.

Another Example:

We recently saw a use case for a handful of investors who wanted to invest in a blockchain company. By pooling their money in a fund, no investor had to commit too much money to the investment and they still met the minimum required investment amount.

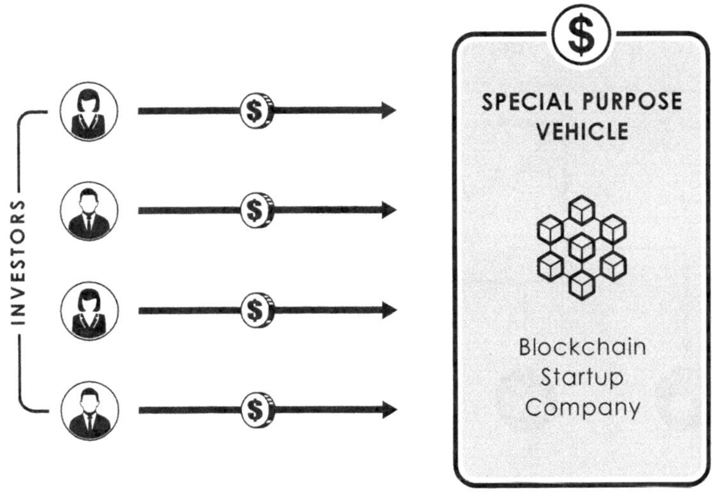

My guess is that you have come across these types of opportunities often and have just let them pass you by because you didn't know how to get involved. I am sure there are ten times more opportunities in your circle of influence alone—if you just start looking for them.

Venture Capital Fund

Venture capital funds are a subset of private equity investments. Venture capital usually denotes a company at some early stage. Financial technology "Fintech," biological technology "Biotech," agricultural technology "Agtech" are all common names these days, but venture capital can cover any tech or non-tech startup you can imagine. Venture capital funds are an excellent way to take small commitments from investors and sprinkle relatively small, but meaningful, investments across many different companies to spread the fund's risk. Even if only one investment makes it, the fund will likely be successful.

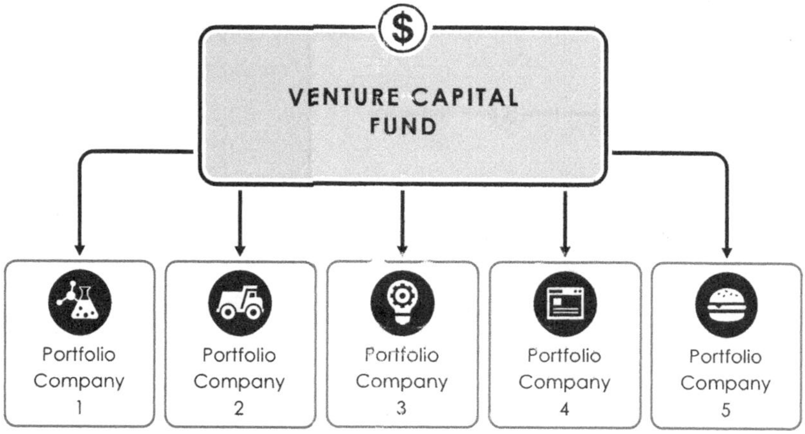

My guess is that you have clients who could help source deals or even own companies themselves that they are building. What a great way to flip the conversation with your clients and stand out!

Example:

A few months ago, one of our clients at Alta Trust emailed me saying that they had a "Big Idea" and wanted to talk it over. They had a strong business and wanted to take it to the next level and in a big way. To do that, they were going to need more capital. They had spoken with several large private equity firms who were interested in investing, but the terms were too rigid. It became obvious that a private fund would allow them to gather the capital they needed and keep the control they desired.

The Leveraged Buyout Fund or Roll-Up Fund

This is the old school private equity approach that targets certain companies in the same industry with the goal of merging them and selling the combined company. The best industries for this type of strategy are usually fragmented without a dominant player or players. The general partner will usually negotiate with mom-and-pop companies and make multiple acquisitions with the intent to combine them and create efficiencies and market dominance, then sell them off. These types of funds have been used many times in all sorts of industries such as pet supply companies, CPA firms, registered investment advisers, garbage companies, auto collision shops, etc. If you happen to target companies under $20 million in value, you could layer on the SBIC approach.

Did you know that many household names are the product of private equity roll-up strategies? Waste Management, Kraft Foods (Mondelez International), AutoNation all came to us from roll-up strategies.

Buyout Fund

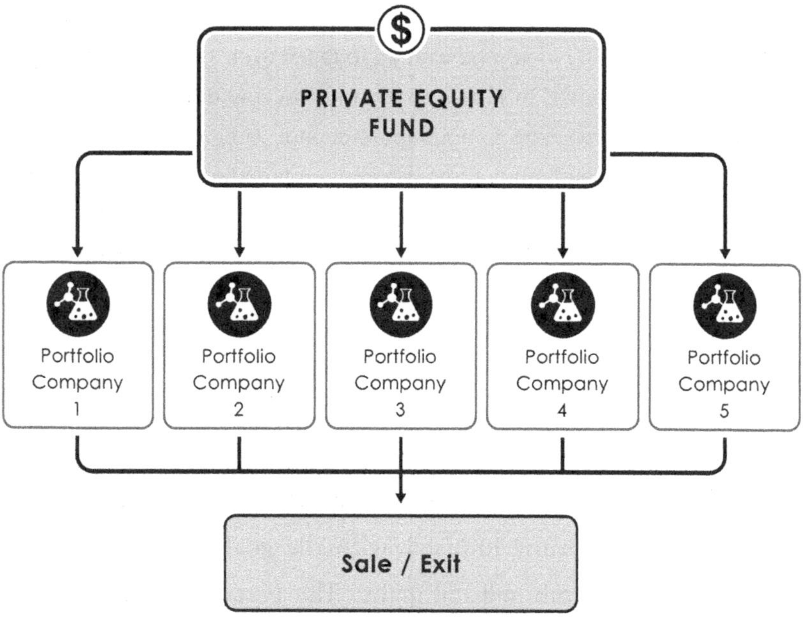

The King of the Community Fund

If I could go back in time to when I was an adviser, I would use this private fund approach. Every adviser should seek to do something like this. Here is how it works.

The adviser creates a private equity fund and structures it such that a substantial percentage (i.e., 75% – 100%) will be invested in the community where they live. They recruit some of the city's most influential and expert individuals to serve on the fund's advisory committee, which will help determine the investments that the fund will make (think *Shark Tank*, but friendlier). You may want to have anywhere from three to five people on the committee, including yourself. Some good candidates tend to be CPAs, attorneys, real estate developers, business owners, etc. Ideally, these individuals help fundraise as well. It becomes an excellent opportunity to be introduced to their friends and associates and expand your connections and influence in the community. What's even better about this approach is that you don't even have to raise a lot of money to make it successful. Depending on the size of a community, a $5 million fund can have a huge impact. Remember you can always create a second fund that will be even bigger and better than the first.

Once capital for the fund is raised, you get to put it to work. Here you have another opportunity to get to know others in the community that you want to meet. Cash is king and you have a lot of it now. What CEO wouldn't at least entertain a discussion for a cash infusion of some sort? What mayor wouldn't carve out time to discuss helping you put this money to work in their community? You just created your own key to the city! Everyone will know you and you will know everyone. Most of all, you will be known as someone who is loyal to your community and people love that. Your investors will likely be part of the community and not only will they love the returns (hopefully), but they will also love that they are doing good for their neighbors. They will be thrilled to eat in a restaurant that they invested in or drive over a bridge they helped finance. Talk about meeting all the needs of an investor—this approach does it all!

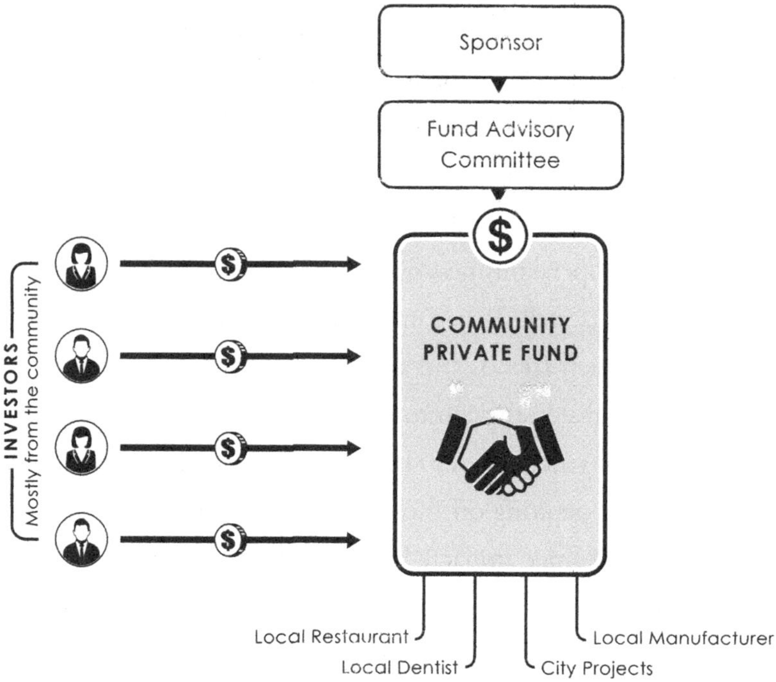

This approach first came up for me when a municipality was looking into the idea of creating a fund themselves.

Another twist on this approach would be to call up the former mayor of your city or another prominent and well-connected person and create a private fund as a joint venture with them, leveraging their reputation.

Combining Bond Separate Accounts into a Private Bond Fund

We talked about combining smaller accounts into a single fund for purposes of avoiding minimum funding requirements. This is the same approach, but for a different reason. If you are an adviser who manages bonds across many separate accounts, you will appreciate the challenges that come with that structure. Because there are new bond issues coming to the market all the time and old bond issues coming off the market just as fast, it can be very difficult for an adviser to keep his separate account portfolios consistent across clients. Managing bonds can be a custom business.

Creating a private fund and combining all the separate accounts into the fund allows greater diversification for the investors and a single simple omnibus account for the adviser to manage. With this approach, every investor participates proportionately in every bond. Investors can contribute their existing bonds to the private fund as an in-kind purchase without creating a taxable event and each investor can retain their current tax basis in the investments — so long as certain requirements are met.

Example:

One of our first private funds fit this mold. An adviser had about $20 million in assets spread across 50 or so separate accounts. Managing the 50 accounts was onerous and scaling the business was not possible. As a result, the adviser asked us to create a single private fund where the bond portfolios could be contributed in kind, providing ease of management for the adviser and increased diversification for the investors.

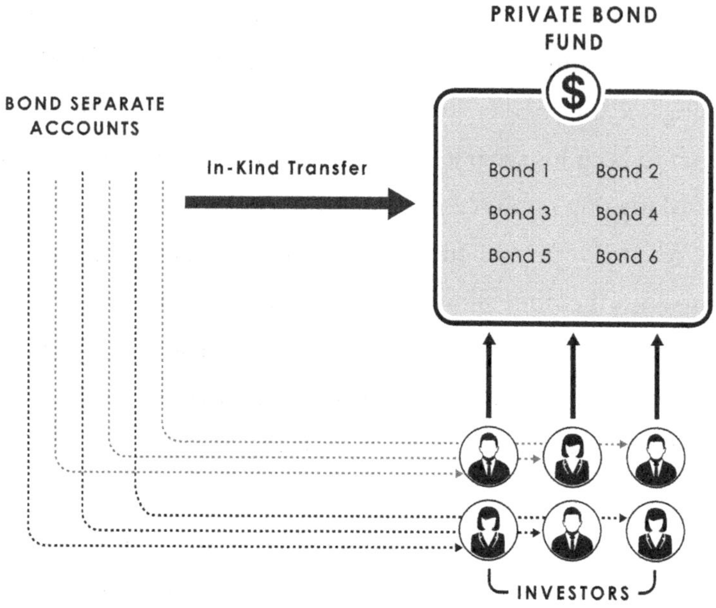

A Structured Note Private Fund

The main impetus for creating a private fund around structured notes is typically diversification for investors and control for the adviser. Because structured notes usually require an investment of $250,000 or $500,000, many advisers' clients may only hold one, two or three notes. The lack of diversification is a problem.

The double benefit of a private fund here is that the investors can have a diverse portfolio of structured products and the adviser can manage the portfolio at their discretion, without having to get pre-approval from any one client.

Example:

This situation came up with an adviser named Jill, who was just going independent and used structured notes often in client portfolios. As her horizons were broadening more generally as an adviser, she realized that her clients could benefit by pooling the structured notes together for diversification. This would allow Jill to make quick investment decisions when opportunities arose that would benefit all her clients together.

Individual Accounts vs. Private Fund

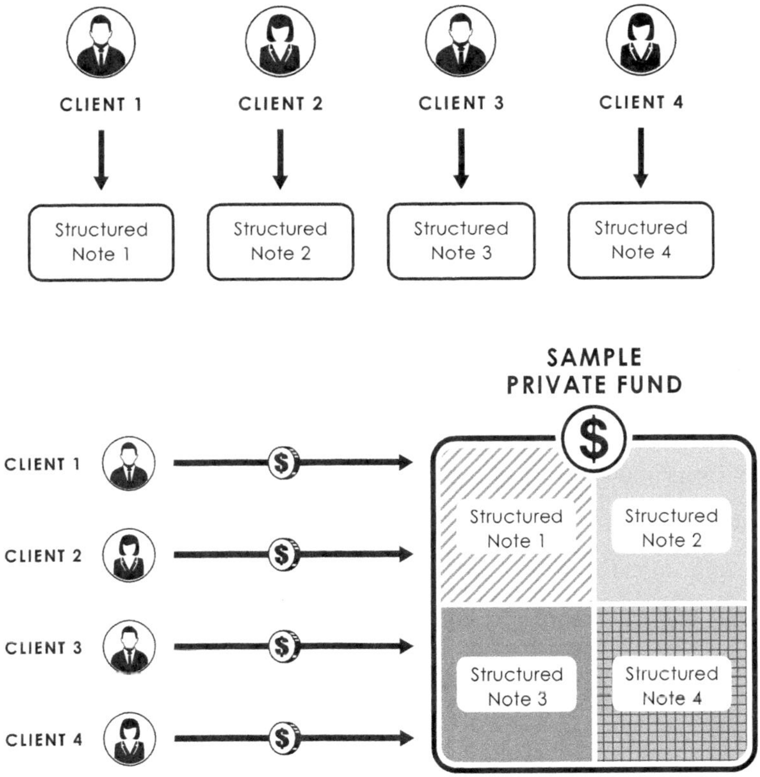

Sponsor Exit and Roll-Up Fund

This approach is a takeoff from the traditional buyout fund. It can be a great way for a sponsor to not only exit their own company, but magnify that exit by adding a roll-up to it. I will use an RIA as an example here, but this approach can work across industries. Here is how you could do it.

Example:

"The Big RIA" is worth $10 million. The Big RIA owner decides to sponsor a private fund called "The RIA Exit Fund" and transfer his ownership of The Big RIA into the The RIA Exit Fund. The sponsor also raises capital for The RIA Exit Fund from outside investors and buys other RIAs within the fund or convinces them to join with an in-kind purchase. After five years, the sponsor has created a much larger RIA and the value of the sponsor's original in-kind contribution has increased to $15 million. Not only that, but the sponsor has been able to charge 2% on the investor capital and will receive 20% of the profits on the investor money.

A few considerations on this approach. First, the in-kind transfer of The Big RIA into the fund will not likely trigger a taxable event; however, the sponsor will maintain the same cost basis and pay taxes accordingly when it is time to exit. Second, be careful to disclose any actual or potential conflicts of interest. And finally, don't do anything like this unless you are willing to sell. Private funds are not designed to go on indefinitely.

The Coat Tails Fund

Do you know someone who has a knack for success? Every time you talk to them, they are either wrapping up or starting up another deal and you just don't know how they do it. Maybe you are that person? Here is what to do.

Example:

I had a conversation not too long ago with a real estate investor who had done quite well for himself. In the past, he had only invested his own money but shared that his friends and acquaintances always asked to co-invest with him. He had no incentive to let them. From his point of view, there was only downside risk in the event that an investment didn't work out. Between the risk and the extra work it would create for him, he always turned his friends down.

The solution was a private fund. With a private fund, he could invest his own money either in the private fund or alongside it. He could easily add outside money in the fund, which would allow him to charge a management fee and take a performance allocation. Now he had an incentive to accept money from other investors.

Your Own M&A Division Fund

A lot of larger companies have entire divisions that are focused on mergers and acquisitions. You may not have the luxury of having access to enough capital to finance such an operation . . . or do you?

Example:

The industry climate is just right for a company to take advantage of the opportunity to purchase competitors, so it creates a private fund that lends money to the company to fund the acquisition. In return, the private fund investors receive interest payments of 8% which are secured by the private fund. Yield is hard to find these days and it could make a lot of sense for the right investor profile.

Variation: You could create a private fund that lends money to multiple companies and only seeks income.

If you use this approach, just make sure to work with your attorney to disclose everything — particularly if you are sponsoring the fund and your fund is borrowing the money.

The Match Made in Heaven Fund, Part 1

It's possible that you are disheartened as your read through these possibilities. Perhaps you can raise capital from investors, but you don't have any investments, or vice versa. Don't worry, this approach is for you.

Example:

Julia can raise the money and Josh has the investment expertise. The two of them create a separate sponsoring entity (usually a limited liability company (LLC)) that will sponsor the new private fund. The LLC will allow Julia and Josh flexibility in how they share management fees and performance fees, and now they have an offering that neither of them could have accomplished on their own.

Variation: Even if you can't raise capital or don't have an investment idea, you can still make this work if you can find others who can. There is value in making the connections and you can create a 3-way partnership by connecting the right people and still cutting yourself into the deal.

As you can see, the private fund opportunities are only limited by your imagination and creativity. Regardless of the structure you select, your clients and their friends will appreciate an adviser offering them the magic of exclusivity and your brand will expand.

Match Made in Heaven Fund, Part 2

Let's take this approach in another direction.

Example:

Kyle is friends with the founder of an exciting new company, "ExciteCo," that is looking for funding and he wants to be a part of it. Kyle tells his friend that he will secure funding for the company, but needs an exclusive agreement. The founder agrees and Kyle goes to work. Kyle knows he can't raise all the money on his own, so he approaches two other associates who can help. Together, they create "NewCo LLC" and sponsor a special purpose vehicle NewCo Private Fund. Kyle and his new partners use their contacts to raise the money in the NewCo Private Fund, which then makes the investment in ExciteCo.

The partners of NewCo LLC share fees in proportion to the money that each raised and, hopefully, the investors in NewCo Private Fund have a great investment.

Variation: NewCo Private Fund was structured such that the five years of management fees (2%) payable to NewCo LLC as sponsor were charged up front. The NewCo LLC partners divide up the proceeds immediately, without having to wait to get paid. This approach feels more like a commission, but it is not—it is merely prepaid management fees and does not require a broker/dealer registration. The fees collected are exclusively management fees that can appropriately be paid out to the fund sponsor and ultimately to the sponsor's partners. Any performance allocations that NewCo LLC is owed will come later.

The Semi-Retired Private Fund

Private funds are a great way to leverage the sage experience and contacts of an industry veteran without their having to put in long work weeks like they used to. Here is how it could work:

Example:

Mary sold her very successful RIA five years ago. She has enjoyed the slower pace since the sale, but has concluded that she is not ready to be truly retired. Mary has maintained her contacts in the industry and now her non-compete agreement is about to expire.

Mary decides to jump back into the industry by sponsoring a private fund with the purpose of rolling up other RIAs. With the capital she has raised, she hires the staff to keep herself to reasonable hours.

The Crypto Fund

Bitcoin and other cryptocurrencies and block chain technologies have been very popular over the last few years. PwC's May 2020 report on crypto hedge funds gives us some interesting market data:

Average crypto fund size:	*$44.4 million*
Average Returns of Most Common Crypto Strategies	
Quantitative:	58%
Long-only return:	42%
Long-short return:	33%
Multi-Strategy:	19%
Average Fees	
Management:	2.3%
Performance:	21.1%

The Gasoline Strategy

Here I am not talking about burning anything to the ground, rather I want you to use this approach to accelerate your growth! 29% of small businesses fail because they run out of cash, but how many don't thrive because they lack the necessary capital? This approach is really at the heart of private equity.

Example:

You know the owner of a very popular restaurant. Your private equity fund takes a minority interest in the restaurant and provides operating capital to help the restaurant expand to several other locations.

Variation: You can use this approach to raise capital for your own company through an SPV structure. This way, investors are indirectly invested in your company. You might offer preferred stock, debt or equity; but because you are the sponsor, you can limit the investors' control over your business by using the private fund as a buffer. Just make sure you are clear with your investors of the potential conflicts and other issues.

Isn't it exciting to see all the possibilities? I love seeing what advisers come up with when it comes to structures. I have been very impressed — there are some incredibly smart advisers out there.

Key Points

1. Private funds are powerful when you know how to use them.
2. There are many ways to use private funds to help your clients and make the world better.
3. You can combine elements of any of these strategies to come up with a private fund offering that suits your situation.

Exercise: After reading the many use cases presented here, ask yourself which one intrigues you the most. Begin thinking through the following questions:

1. Would I partner with someone on this private fund? If yes, who?
2. Who do I know that would like to invest?
3. Who do I know who is connected to others who may want to invest?
4. Do I have one or two potential target investments?

6

Private Fund Fees and Expenses

CHARGING FEES IS A FAIRLY SIMPLE CONCEPT AND MOST ADvisers are accustomed to charging a basis point fee for their services at the end of each month or quarter. You may choose to make the fees in your private fund simple, but because of the increased flexibility, fees often become much more complicated than a traditional asset management fee in a separate account.

Private Equity Style Fees

Private equity funds have a very distinct structure for charging fees, so for clarity I am keeping the private equity and hedge fund fee models separate. Real estate funds may charge fees more like one or the other or even a hybrid of the two.

Private Equity Management Fees

Almost every PE Fund has a management fee that is paid to the sponsor. Management fees can vary significantly, but generally fall between 1% and 3% for private equity.

Because PE funds secure commitments and call down capital as needed, a sponsor will charge a management fee on either "committed capital" (all of the commitments regardless of funding) or on "called capital" (only capital received into the fund). In the past, it was more common for sponsors to charge on committed capital, but now it is more commonplace for general partners to only charge on called capital. One other difference with PE funds is that they may choose to charge different management fees based on the stage of the fund.

Private Equity Fund Management Fees

Example 1

- 2% management fee on all "committed capital."

Example 2

- 2% management fee on all "called capital."

Example 3

- 2% of "called capital" through the investment period;
- 1% through the exit period;
- 0% during any applicable extension period.

Some RIAs find the concept of charging a management fee on a fixed asset amount (e.g., called capital) unusual. They are accustomed to charging on the market value of a portfolio at the end of the month or quarter. The structure makes sense when you consider that a PE fund will lose money initially (remember the J Curve), and then hopefully exponentially increase over the life of the fund. The purpose of the management fee is for the sponsor to pay their employees, office space and generally keep the lights on while they manage the fund. Sponsors typically make most of their money from the performance allocation, which is where they can participate in the fund's growth. Management fees may be paid in advance or in arrears, in accordance with the valuation date of the fund.

Performance Allocations (Carried Interest)

Performance allocations (also referred to as carried interest), performance fees, performance bonuses or incentive fees, are very common in private funds. We always recommend referring to them in offering documents as "performance allocations" for tax and accounting reasons. Many investors like the fact that the general partner has a strong incentive to perform well and is willing to pay a performance allocation. Here is a simplified example of a common scenario of a performance allocation.

EXAMPLE: ABC PRIVATE FUND	
Fund Inception – Invested Capital	$100 million
Fund Exit – Total Proceeds	$150 million
Sponsor's Performance Allocation 20% of $50 million	$10 million
Distributable Assets to Investors	**$140 million**

In some cases, a performance allocation may be tiered. For instance: 20% of profits generally, but if the fund returns over 100% during a period, the performance allocation could be 30%.

Preferred Return (Hurdle Rate)

A hurdle rate, also referred to as a preferred return, is another way of protecting an investor. It means that the fund returns must be above a certain threshold before the sponsor is eligible to receive a performance allocation. That threshold is usually a percentage, such as 8%. PE funds traditionally use a fixed percentage or prime plus a percentage. The key is to choose a hurdle rate that doesn't provide any confusion or have the possibility of manipulating. This is where it is also helpful to have a third-party fund administrator who can calculate the returns and apply the hurdle rate independently. Hurdle rates are common in both hedge funds and private equity funds. High water marks generally do not apply to PE funds.

Distribution Waterfall

The calculation and payout of a fund's proceeds between the investors and the sponsor is referred to as a distribution waterfall. Though waterfall models may be customized, there are generally four components in a distribution waterfall.

1. **Return of capital** - 100% of distributions goes to the investors until investors recover all invested capital.

2. **Preferred return** - 100% of further distributions goes to investors until they receive the stated preferred return on their investment.

3. **Sponsor catch-up** - 100% of the next tranche of distributions goes to the general partner of the fund to put them in parity with the investors, based on the preferred return.

4. **The Profit Split** - The investors and sponsor each receive their respective allocations of the remaining profits.

For a PE fund, a sponsor may choose either the European-style waterfall (Whole of Fund) or the American-style waterfall (Deal by Deal). The European-style waterfall is applied across all the fund's investments at the end of the life of the fund. American-style means that the distribution waterfall is applied each time a portfolio company is exited.

In the European-style, the sponsor must wait until the end of the fund to receive any profit allocations. In the American-style, the sponsor will get paid sooner, but if they receive a performance allocation on the first deal exit and then the second deal exit is at a loss, they could be required to pay some or all of their performance fees back to the investors, often referred to as a "clawback." Most private equity funds using the American-style method hold back some of their profit allocations in an escrow account for that reason.

Hedge Fund Style Fees

The hedge fund approach to fees will feel much more familiar to registered investment advisers.

Management Fees

Hedge fund management fees typically range between 1% and 2% of the fund's assets. The management fee calculation in a hedge fund is very similar to what most advisers are accustomed to. The fee is based on a percentage of the market value of the fund at the end of a period (e.g., month-end). Management fees may be charged either in advance or in arrears.

Performance Allocations (Incentive Fees)

Performance allocations in a hedge fund are a straightforward split, based on the fund meeting certain requirements. Because most hedge funds are continuously offered and there is no end date, the performance allocation for a hedge fund is calculated and accrued upon each valuation period (e.g., monthly) and crystalized (or realized) annually. Once a performance allocation is crystalized and paid out, the performance calculation resets for the next year.

Hurdle Rate (Preferred Return)

Just like a hurdle rate in a PE fund, hedge funds will often subject their performance allocations to a hurdle rate. Hedge funds commonly use a standard benchmark, such as the S&P 500, as the hurdle to beat.

High-Water Marks

The concept of a high-water mark is simple. The high-water mark is the highest value of the fund. It is used to ensure that fund sponsors do not receive a performance allocation for poor performance and prevents a sponsor from receiving a performance allocation on the same performance twice. A fund with a high-water mark provision protects investors and only allows a sponsor to receive a performance allocation if there is an absolute increase in the value of the fund.

Private Fund Revenue/Return Example

1% Management Fee • 10% Performance Allocation • 12% Annual Returns

Investor Returns

Percentage:	60%
Dollar:	$17,877,664

Sponsor Fees

Management Fee:	$1,824,251
Performance Allocation:	$2,189,102
Total:	**$4,013,353**

Dollar Growth by Year

Beginning Capital Year 1:	$30,000,000
Beginning Capital Year 2:	$32,940,000
Beginning Capital Year 3:	$36,168,120
Beginning Capital Year 4:	$39,712,596
Beginning Capital Year 5:	$43,604,430

Additional Fee Considerations

Fee Waivers and Side Letter

Sponsors usually retain the right in the fund offering documents to waive all or a portion of their fees to an investor or investors. It is common for an anchor or key investor to receive special treatment when it comes to fees. This usually comes in the form of a side letter arrangement documenting the agreement. The sponsor has the latitude to make those concessions as they choose. In some cases, a side letter may also address liquidity or other preferences.

Share Classes

If there will be a group of investors that will need the same fee or term concessions, then a special share class may be a better option than managing many side letters. One example might be a zero-fee share class for investors who are already being charged an advisory fee from the adviser. Another example could be a reduced management fee for a larger investment. A new share class does not increase the number of investors you can have in a fund.

Share Classes Examples

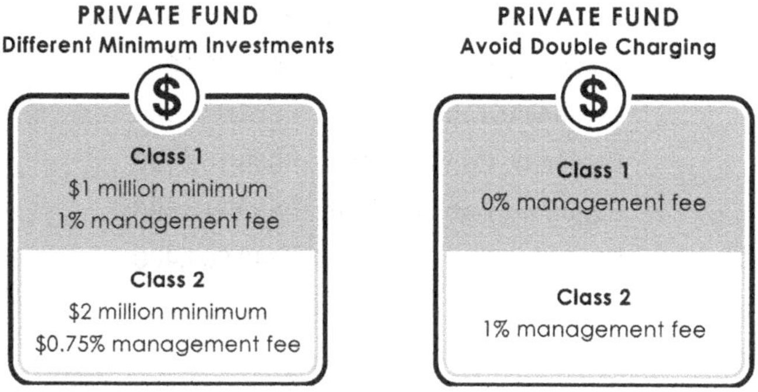

Private Fund Expenses

All expenses are charged to the fund. It is rare for a sponsor to pay for fund expenses and not be reimbursed by the fund. There are occasions when a general partner might subsidize a fund, but that is the exception and most frequently seen if the manager bears the organization costs to get the fund up and running. Below is a list of most of the expenses — they may or may not apply, depending on the fund.

Fund Establishment Costs

Most securities law firms will charge between $50,000 and $300,000 to create private fund offering documents. Depending on the complexity of a fund, it could be more; but I would be even more wary about paying less. No matter how simple or easy you think your structure is, you want it to be set up correctly.

At Alta Trust, we have worked with top attorneys to create excellent draft offering documents that we can customize for our clients. With these draft documents as a foundation, the adviser can work with their own securities and investment adviser counsel to ensure that the offering is tailored to them and their situation. Using this approach, our adviser clients save tens, if not hundreds, of thousands of dollars.

I feel bad every time we speak to a firm who just went through the time and expense of creating their fund from scratch prior to talking with us. Inevitably, they have spent between $50,000 and $300,000 in legal expenses alone.

On the flip side, I cringe any time I speak to someone who "has a brother-in-law who is an attorney" who wrote up their offering documents. There are so many potential ways for that to go badly!

Not only do our adviser partners receive a great foundation for their offering documents, but we are also able to guide and consult them along the way on the more practical aspects of owning and operating a private fund.

Most offering documents provide for the payment of establishment or organizational costs. This often comes in the form of a reimbursement to the sponsor who paid the upfront costs to bring the fund to launch. The sponsor can be reimbursed by the fund if it does not materially hurt the fund investors. In other words, depending on the size of the fund and the amount of the establishment costs, the reimbursement may come all at once or over time.

Administration

Selecting the right administrator will be one of the most important decisions you make regarding your fund. It will be the difference between smooth sailing and massive headaches. You should select a firm with the right experience, systems and personnel to make everything run smoothly. The last thing you want to do is go back to your investors and take the blame for a mistake made by your administrator. You can expect both establishment and ongoing charges based on the work you engage them to do.

At our firm, fund administration includes:

- **Interest Owner / Limited Partner Accounting**
  - ☑ Issue purchase/redemption confirmations to investors upon acceptance of subscriptions and/or redemptions by the sponsor and/or the fund
  - ☑ Calculate capital calls/drawdowns and prepare and issue the capital call/funding notices to the investors

- ☑ Calculate distributions and prepare and issue the distribution notices to the investors
- ☑ Prepare capital account statements to investors upon each valuation period
- ☑ Record capital activity of each investor
- ☑ Prepare quarterly profit-and-loss allocation for investors

Fund Accounting

- ☑ Record cash flows and reconcile to the general ledger
- ☑ Record sponsor-provided valuations for the portfolio investments
- ☑ Value the fund quarterly in accordance with the organizational and offering documents
- ☑ Calculate the preferred return (hurdle rate), if applicable, for the investors and calculate any performance allocation to the sponsor
- ☑ Administer multiple fee classes, as applicable

Reporting

- ☑ Quarterly unaudited Financial Statements (includes Statement of Assets, Liabilities and Investors' Capital, Schedule of Investments, Statement of Operations, Statement of Changes in Investors' Capital, Statement of Cash Flows)
- ☑ Investor Capital Account Statements

☑ Valuation Reports, including by way of example:

- Valuation Summary
- Trial Balance
- General Ledger
- Capital Accounts (broken out by investor)
- Capital Activity (high-level summary)
- Bank and Cash Reconciliation
- Portfolio Investments
- Accruals
- Expenses
- Preferred Return (hurdle rate)
- Carried Interest/Performance Allocation
- High-water Mark
- Quarter-to-date Cost Rollforward
- Year-to-date Cost Rollforward
- Inception-to-date Cost Rollforward

☑ Support annual audit and prepare draft financial statements with footnotes.

☑ Support annual tax return and Form K-1 preparation

☑ 1099 preparation

Compliance

Getting compliance right is a must. If you fall down here, your fund may never get up again and it could affect your ability to raise money for future funds. There are all sorts of pitfalls that can potentially go wrong that may result in fines, integration, registration as a mutual fund and lawsuits. Ultimately, the general partner is responsible for compliance. They need to hire competent auditors, accountants and legal counsel, and maybe even outsource compliance for the fund. Regardless, the general partner should have an internal compliance program and a head of compliance to ensure the program is followed. According to a KPMG report, compliance accounts for 7% of a fund's expenses and this amount is growing as the industry continues to get serious about compliance. At Alta Trust, we assist many of our fund sponsors with basic compliance services, but everything is done under the direction and approval of the sponsor.

At Alta Trust, we assist in the following areas of compliance:

1. Preparing and filing required federal and state securities notices
2. Performing anti-money laundering and anti-terrorism checks through government lists such as OFAC and FinCEN
3. Monitoring the investor count for the fund
4. Monitoring the fund's ERISA status

While these are all important and fundamental compliance items, there are many other considerations. You can visit **www.privatefundsmadesimple.com** to obtain a checklist of compliance items you should consider before starting a private fund.

Custodian

Having an independent custodian for a fund can provide a lot of assurance to investors and potential protection to a registered adviser from being deemed a custodian. Costs range from flat dollars to basis point charges on assets under custody (most common). The institutional custodian provides third-party reporting on the assets. At Alta Trust, included in our business trust structures, we also serve as custodian to the fund assets.

Prime Broker

A hedge fund will need to engage a prime broker that will facilitate the sponsor's trading activities. In a business trust structure, to facilitate Alta Trust taking custody, the account would be set up in the name of Alta Trust for the benefit of the hedge fund. The prime broker may charge transaction or basis points to the account for its services. If other outside brokers are used for trade execution, they will charge a transaction fee as well.

Placement Agents

If a fund uses a placement agent to raise capital, either the sponsor or the investor may pay the fee. The charge may come in the form of a commission based on the investment amounts they place, similar to a loaded mutual fund. Or the charge may be paid out of the sponsor's fee, which is more advantageous to investors. Placement agents may require a retainer and typically charge between 1% and 2.5% of capital raised. The placement agent must be registered as or with a broker/dealer.

Audit and Tax

A fund audit is important if you are trying to raise assets beyond a "friends and family" fund. Audits range in price, but usually start around $15,000 annually for a reputable firm. The fund tax return preparation and K-1 preparation usually starts at $7,500. Both depend on the size of the fund, number of investors and the overall complexity of the fund.

Legal

It is best if the fund has its own legal counsel. For most funds that we support, this will not likely be a large expense unless there is litigation, but it is important to have good counsel to help the fund avoid problems and interpret gray areas.

Borrowing

If your fund uses margin, lines of credit or mortgages while investing, you should factor in the cost of borrowing.

Securities Pricing

For publicly traded securities such as stocks, exchange-traded funds and mutual funds, the pricing of securities is nominal, especially if a fund is valued only once a month or quarter. The costs from the industry-standard providers tend to be around two to five cents per security price. Bonds, mortgage-backed securities and other more complicated securities may be as high as $3 per security. There is also a cost for corporate action reporting such as dividends, interest, stock splits, etc. For private and illiquid assets, you may choose to hire an appraiser or business valuation specialist, although it is not required. This approach will add a more significant expense burden to the fund.

Bank Fees

Each fund will have an operating account in order to process subscriptions and redemptions, and pay expenses and fees. The fees generally include items such as wire transfers, ACH, account fees, etc.

Regulatory Filings

A private fund must submit several filings: the initial entity creation, Form Reg D, state or blue sky filings, etc. Most of these filings require payment.

Miscellaneous Expenses

Real estate and private equity funds will incur many other costs such as maintenance, appraisals, development, taxes, etc. Sometimes sponsors will charge travel, marketing and other expenses to the fund as well.

You need to be aware of all the fees before you get started. These fees must be clearly disclosed to your investors and agreed to up front. It's your job to make it an attractive investment, even with the costs of running the fund properly.

Fees and expenses are just part of the private fund opportunity. By taking the time to find the right partners to help you put your fund together, you can minimize the fund expenses and maximize your fund's chances for success.

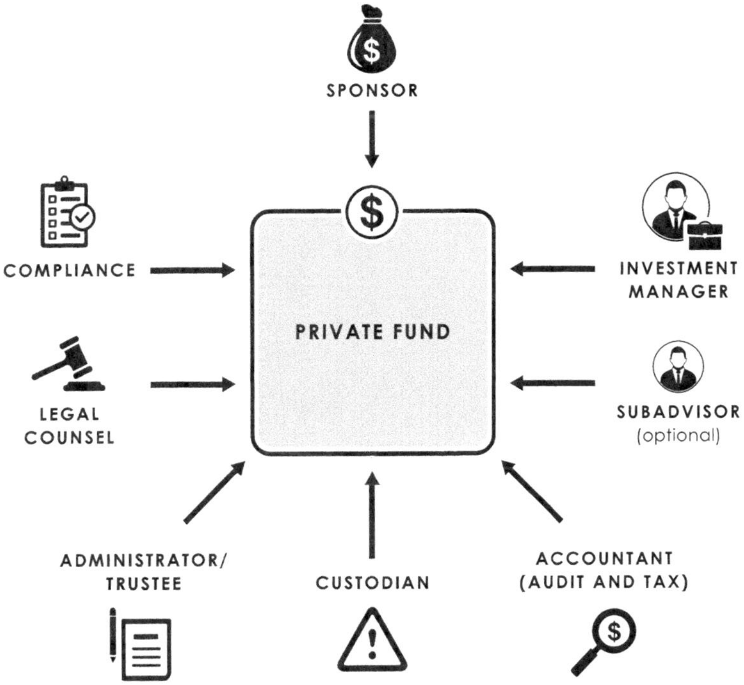

At this point, you may be wondering what size fund makes sense in order to support the fund expenses and still be a good investment for the investors. Based on our experience and our fees and expenses at Alta Trust, the following asset ranges are good minimum targets to have in mind.

WHEN DOES A FUND MAKE SENSE?	
Fund Type	**Minimum Asset Size**
Special Purpose Vehicle	$5 – 10 million
Private Equity Fund	$10 – 15 million
Real Estate Fund	$10 – 15 million
Hedge Fund	$15 – 20 million

Key Points

1. Private equity funds and hedge funds charge fees differently.
2. Private funds can be very lucrative for fund sponsors.
3. Make sure you have accounted for all potential costs ahead of time.
4. Ensure that the investment will likely be good for investors in consideration of the fund expenses.

7

Private Fund Laws, Rules and Regulations

WHEN I LAUNCHED MY FIRST PRIVATE FUND, I WAS SURPRISED to learn how many laws, rules and regulations there were, and the industry has only become more complicated since that time. There are federal and state rules that need to be followed. There are also exemptions to those rules that have certain requirements if you want to qualify. Navigating the regulatory maze can be difficult. My goal in this chapter is to save you a lot of time and money by giving you a bird's eye view of private fund regulations.

The 1933 Securities Act ('33 Act)

The 1933 Securities Act ('33 Act) was passed after the stock market crash of 1929 with the dual goals of providing investors more transparency and creating laws against misrepresentation and fraud in the securities markets. The '33 Act requires that investors have standard financial information prior to offering securities for sale.

Essentially, the '33 Act is focused on security transactions or, in other words, buying and selling securities. The '33 Act does provide for certain exemptions and the SEC has formalized those in Regulation D.

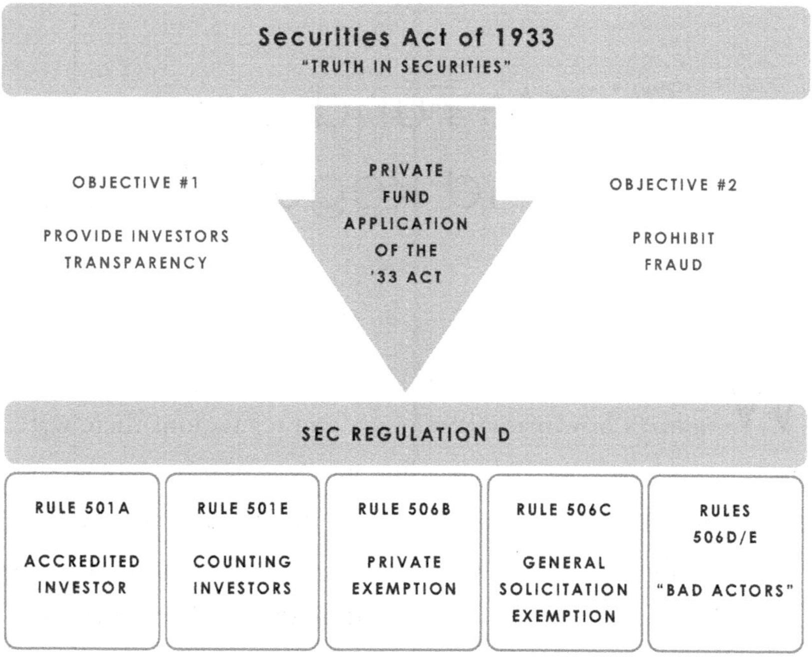

The '33 Act requires that all securities be registered with the SEC. Fortunately, there are some exceptions to the registration requirement, which are:

- Private offerings to a limited number of persons or institutions
- Offerings of limited size
- Intrastate offerings
- Securities of municipal, state and federal governments

Regulation D

I am sure you have heard the term Reg D frequently throughout your career. Regulation D was adopted by the SEC to provide further clarification on how to meet the requirements for an exempt offering. If you are going to launch a private fund, it is important for you to comply with Reg D to the letter. Even with a properly filed and followed Reg D fund, you will not be exempt from the anti-fraud, civil liability or other provisions of the federal securities laws. In addition, you must also comply with applicable state laws for each investor's state of residence.

There are too many variables to address every state or other exemptions here, so I will only address the most commonly used rules under Reg D.

- **Rule 501a** - definition of an accredited investor
- **Rule 501e** - describes the process for counting investors
- **Rule 506b** - private solicitation safe harbor
- **Rule 506c** - general solicitation safe harbor
- **Rules 506d/e** - "bad actor" disqualification and disclosure

Reg D: Rule 501a "The Accredited Investor"

We will discuss this in more detail later, but private funds are only to be offered to accredited investors.

As of December 8, 2020, an accredited investor is defined by the SEC as one of the following:

- Any bank
- Any registered broker/dealer
- Any registered investment adviser
- Any '40 Act fund
- Any insurance company
- Any small business investment company
- Any employee benefit plan, 501c3 organization, partnership, trust, family office, Native American tribe with over $5 million in assets
- Any director, executive officer or general partner of the issuer of securities
- Any person whose individual net worth or joint net worth with that person's spouse or spousal equivalent exceeds $1 million (not including primary residence)
- Any person whose individual income exceeds $200,000 in each of the two most recent years or whose joint income with that person's spouse or spousal equivalent exceeds $300,000 in each of those years, and has a reasonable expectation of reaching the same income in the current year
- Any entity in which all the equity owners are accredited investors
- Any person holding in good standing one or more professional certifications designated by the SEC, which as of February 1, 2021, means Series 7, Series 65 and Series 82 licenses
- Any knowledgeable employee of the issuer

Reg D: Rule 501e "Counting Investors"

It is important to count the investors in a fund properly. The last thing you want to do is lose your exemption. I will provide an overview of the methodology, but I recommend engaging a professional to help with this to avoid any trouble or confusion. Counting investors may be more complicated than you think.

▶ Individuals

Individuals are counted as single investors. Relatives, spouses or spousal relatives who share the same primary address are all considered to be the same investor. Any corporation or entity in which an individual owns more than 50% of the equity or a trust or estate in which they have more than 50% of the beneficial interest would not be counted as an additional investor.

▶ Entities

Corporations, partnerships, etc., are counted as single investors unless:

1. The entity is organized for the specific purpose of acquiring the securities (then all the shareholders of the entity are counted), or
2. The entity owns more than 10% of the fund's assets (in which case there is a look-through to the entity shareholders and they are all included in the count).

▶ Retirement Plans

A non-contributory employee benefit plan, such as a defined benefit plan, is counted as a single investor as long as it is the trustee who makes all investment decisions for the plan.

▶ Trusts

Trusts are usually considered to be one investor, particularly if there is a trustee making the investment decisions on behalf of the trust.

▶ The General Partner

It is common for general partners to invest in their own funds. Investors like to know that they are in the same boat with the general partner. General partners do not take up any investor spots and are not counted for the purposes of reaching the total number of 100 investors for a 3c1 fund.

The 10% Look-Through Investor Counting Method

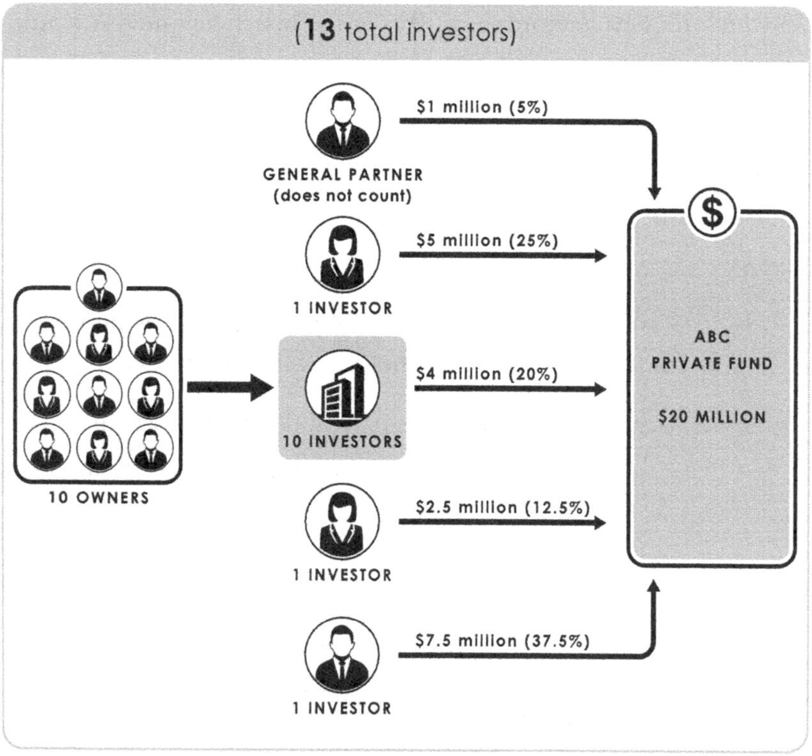

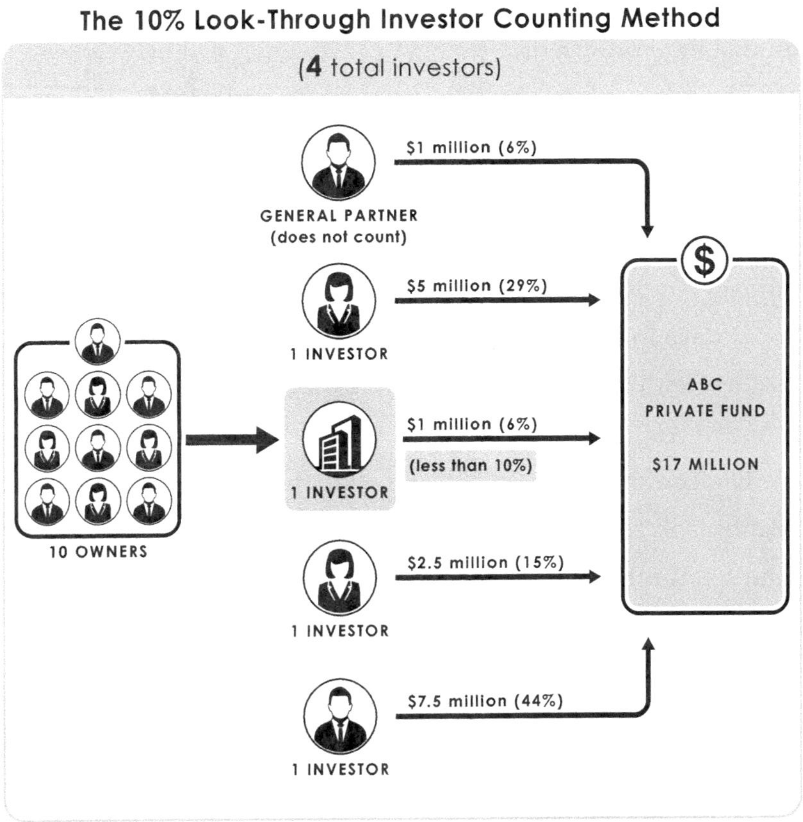

Reg D: Rule 506b "The Private Exemption"

First, any 506b offering must meet all the requirements under 501a, which is the most commonly applicable rule. Rule 501a states that the investors in a fund must generally be accredited. There is an exception for up to 35 non-accredited investors who are considered to be knowledgeable. However, unless the fund is set up for close friends and family, I would highly recommend staying away from non-accredited investors. You take on significantly more risk for a small amount of money. You are also required to provide more financial information and detail on the use of funds (think mutual fund prospectus).

The other important thing to know about a 506b offering is that it **must be private.** You cannot market or publicize the fund in any way. You cannot put the fund on a public website nor can you make the fund known in any other general ways, such as an email campaign or webinar to the public or social media advertising. All prospective investors should be people that you already know, do business with and have a reasonable expectation that they qualify as accredited investors.

Under a 506b offering, the investors must represent that they qualify as accredited investors, but there is no requirement that the fund sponsor must verify the representation unless they have cause for suspicion.

Reg D: Rule 506c "The General Solicitation Exemption"

On April 5, 2012, the Jumpstart our Business startups, also called the "JOBS Act" threw out an 80-year history of not allowing public advertising of a private offering. The legislation instructed the SEC to lift the ban on general solicitations of private offerings, as long as fund sponsors only subscribed accredited investors into the fund and the fund took reasonable steps to verify that the investors were indeed accredited. This is referred to as Rule 506c (general solicitation).

Any fund filing under the 506c exemption can market the fund broadly and publicly. Websites, email campaigns, even television, radio and social media advertising are possible. Essentially, you can advertise the fund to anyone, but only subscribe verified accredited investors. It is important to note that while general solicitation offerings have been available for quite some time, they are yet to be adopted en masse. For those that do choose a 506c offering, make sure you review all the rules and regulations in detail with your securities attorney.

General Solicitation Fund (506c)

The SEC provides examples of ways a fund sponsor might verify a prospective investor's accreditation status. Some of the suggested steps are:

- A review by the fund sponsor of the prospective investor's last two years' tax returns, along with a written statement that they expect to reach the same income for the current year.
- A review by the fund sponsor of current bank statements, brokerage accounts, tax assessments and independent third-party appraisals.
- Liabilities may be checked by the fund sponsor by reviewing a report issued by a nationwide consumer reporting agency.

- The last and most common way is by receiving a written confirmation of their accredited investor status by one of the following:
    - A registered broker/dealer
    - An investment adviser registered with the SEC
    - A licensed attorney who is in good standing under the laws of the jurisdictions in which they are admitted to practice law
    - A certified public accountant who is duly registered and in good standing under the laws of the place of their residence or principal office

Another interesting thing to know is that a fund can elect 506c status at the time of the Reg D filing with the SEC. Once a fund elects 506c status, it can never be revised. However, if the general partner elects the more traditional "private exemption" status under 506b for the fund, then it is possible to update the election to a 506c general solicitation fund at a future time.

Reg D: Rule 506d "Bad Actors"

It may seem fairly obvious that you don't want to have convicted felons running or influencing a private fund investment, but be sure you take this rule seriously. If you avoid going through the documentation process and something comes up down the road with a partner, you can lose your Reg D exemption and cause things to go from bad to worse for your fund quickly.

The basic premise of the rule is that no one who serves the fund as general partner, director, executive officer, affiliate, managing member, solicitor, adviser of the fund or any beneficial owner of the fund who has 20% or more of the outstanding voting rights can answer "yes" to any of the following conditions:

1. Has been convicted of a felony or misdemeanor within the last ten years in connection with the purchase or sale of a security or arising out of the conduct of the business of underwriter, broker, dealer, investment adviser or paid solicitor of purchasers of securities;

2. Is subject to any court order entered within the preceding five years that would prohibit an individual from engaging in the practice of purchasing or selling securities;

3. Is subject to a final order of a state securities commission or a state authority that bars them from being part of a regulated entity or transacting in securities, insurance or banking services; or is subject to any order based on fraudulent activity;

4. Is subject to an order of the SEC that suspends or revokes that person's registration, places limitations on their activities or bars them from participating in penny stocks;

5. Is subject to any order of the SEC entered within five years that orders the person to cease and desist from committing or causing a violation or future violation of the anti-fraud provisions of federal securities laws or the registration of the '33 Act;

6. Is suspended or expelled from membership in, or suspended or barred from association with a member of, a registered national securities exchange or a registered national or affiliated securities association for any act or omission to act constituting conduct inconsistent with just and equitable principles of trade;

7. Has filed (as a registrant or issuer), or was named as an underwriter in, any registration statement or Regulation A offering statement filed with the Commission that, within five years before such sale, was the subject of a refusal order, stop order or order suspending the Regulation A exemption, or is, at the time of such sale, the subject of an investigation or proceeding to determine whether a stop order or suspension order should be issued; or
8. Is subject to a United States Postal Service false representation order entered within the last five years with respect to conduct alleged by the United States Postal Service to constitute a scheme or device for obtaining money or property through the mail by means of false representations.

Reg D: Rule 506e – "Disclosure of Prior 'Bad Actor' Events"

The general partner must issue to each investor within a reasonable time period a description in writing of any matters that would have triggered a bad actor disqualification, but occurred before September 23, 2013. The failure to furnish such information timely shall not prevent an issuer from relying on this section if the issuer establishes that it did not know and, in the exercise of reasonable care, could not have known of the existence of the undisclosed matter or matters.

Your compliance with Reg D under the '33 Act provides an exemption from the securities transactions that you enter into with your investors, but it does not exempt the security itself. For that relief, we must turn our attention to the Investment Company Act of 1940 ('40 Act).

The Investment Company Act of 1940 ('40 Act)

The '40 Act is the federal law that regulates investment pools or funds. The purpose of the '40 Act is to provide some structure and standards for funds in general and to try to keep investors safe. The '40 Act has a broad mandate and covers all entities that issue interests when the entity's principal business is investing, reinvesting and trading securities. If a structure meets these criteria, which most will, it is defined as an investment company and needs to then register as a mutual fund under the '40 Act.

Investment Company Act of 1940

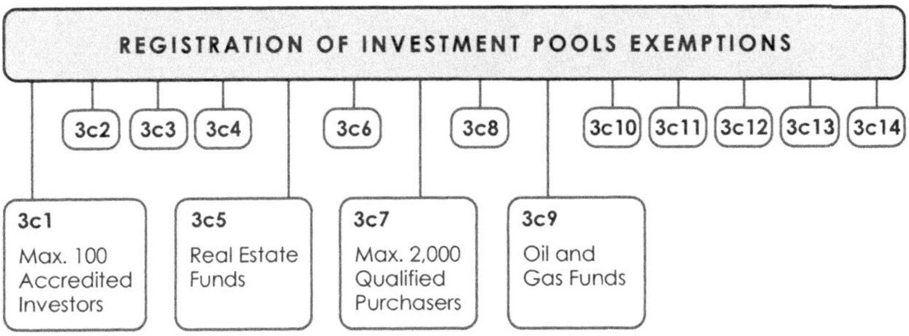

However, like the '33 Act, the '40 Act itself has carved out several exemptions from the law that are important for our discussion. The exemptions are found under Section 3. We will only focus on the four exemptions that are most applicable to this book, but I have included the entire list for your reference. Any fund that can legitimately claim one of the following exemptions does not have to register their fund with the SEC and is therefore not subject to the rigorous rules and expensive regulations that all registered funds must follow.

- **3c1:** *Any issuer whose outstanding securities are not publicly* advertised *and beneficially owned by no more than 100 persons, and those persons must qualify as accredited investors in accordance with Reg D Rule 501a*
- **3c2:** Broker/dealers
- **3c3:** Banks and insurance companies
- **3c4:** Small loan providers and industrial banks
- **3c5:** *Finance companies and lenders secured by real estate*
- **3c6:** Any company primarily engaged directly or through its subsidiaries that falls under exemptions 3(c)(3), 3(c)(4) and 3(c)(5)
- **3c7:** *Any issuer whose securities are not publicly advertised and owned by not more than 2,000 qualified purchasers (QPs)*
- **3c8:** Repealed
- **3c9:** *Any issuer whose primary business consists of owning oil and gas, mineral leases or other similar interests*
- **3c10:** Any company organized for religious, educational or charitable purposes
- **3c11:** Any qualified retirement pension plan, profit sharing plan or collective investment trust sponsored by a bank
- **3c12:** A voting trust for a single issuer
- **3c13:** Any security holder's protective committee which only issues certificates of deposit or short-term paper
- **3c14:** Any church-sponsored plan

The 3c1 Exemption

3cl is the most commonly used exemption for hedge funds and private equity funds. Essentially, to qualify under 3cl, the fund must meet two primary criteria. First, the fund must only take investments from accredited investors. Second, the fund is not allowed to have more than 100 investors.

The 3c7 Exemption

Under the 3c7 exemption, the investor limit is raised substantially from 100 to 2,000. However, the suitability standard is raised significantly as well. Accredited investors must have at least $1 million net worth. A qualified purchaser is defined as a person or entity meeting one of the following requirements:

1. An individual who owns at least $5 million in investments.
2. Any trust which owns at least $5 million in investments and was not formed for the purchase of acquiring the securities offered.
3. Any entity that in the aggregate owns and invests not less than $25 million on a discretionary basis.

Remember that the intent of the 3cl and 3c7 exemptions is to keep the fund offerings private. Even though the 3c7 exemption allows for a much higher number of investors, it is a much more exclusive group that still maintains the non-public nature of these offerings.

It is not uncommon for a 3c7 fund to have minimums as high as $5 or $10 million for a single investment.

3c5 Real Estate Funds

A 3c5 fund is a fund that invests in real estate or real estate-backed securities such as mortgages.

The SEC has a complicated formula for a fund to meet the 3c5 exemption requirements, but generally speaking, a fund must have at least 80% of its total assets consist of qualifying interests (e.g., mortgages) and real estate-type interests; no more than 20% of its total assets may consist of assets that have no relationship to real estate. This is called the "asset composition test."

If a fund qualifies for the 3c5 exemption, it can have an unlimited number of accredited investors in the fund!

3c9 Oil and Gas Funds

The exemption reads:

> "Any person substantially all of whose business consists of owning or holding oil, gas, or other mineral royalties or leases, or fractional interests therein, or certificates of interest or participation in or investment contracts relative to such royalties, leases, or fractional interests."

For a sponsor using this exemption, the fund can have an unlimited number of investors; but like the real estate exemption, they must all be accredited.

Oil and gas funds can come in several forms. I have actually formed and run two different oil and gas funds. Everything about these funds is complicated from finding and securing the deals to managing the day-to-day, not to mention the tax work. That said, one of the main benefits of an oil and gas fund is that investors can receive deductions for both tangible and intangible drilling costs. These deductions are in place to incentivize investors to drill and can be quite substantial. Oil and gas is definitely a boom-or-bust type of an investment, so be careful if you decide to invest in something like this and make sure you have partners or consultants who have a lot of experience.

TABLE OF SUITABILITY				
	Non-RIA Sponsored Fund with a Performance Allocation	RIA Sponsored Fund with a Performance Allocation	3c1 Fund (up to 100 Investors)	3c7 Fund (up to 2,000 Investors)
Accredited ($1 million net worth individual/ $5 million entity)	✓	✗	✓	✗
Qualified Client ($2.1 million net worth)	✓	✓	✓	✗
Qualified Purchaser ($5 million investible assets - individual/ $25 million entity	✓	✓	✓	✓

INVESTOR TYPES		
Non-Accredited	**Accredited Individuals (AIs)**	**Accredited Institutions (AIs)**
May be one of 35 investors in a 3c1 fund with heightened disclosures	May invest in a 3c1 fund	May invest in a 3c1 fund
Any person or entity who does not meet the definition of Accredited Investor	$1 million in net worth (not including principal residence)	Any bank, insurance company, registered broker/dealer or registered investment adviser, exempt reporting advisers
	or	Any of the following entities with at least $5 million in assets; Corporations, LLCs, Partnerships, Trusts, Family Offices, Funds, Indian Tribes, 501c3, Governmental Bodies, Foreign Entities
	$200k in income for the previous 2 years	Any entity in which all of the equity owners are accredited investors
	or	
	$300k of income per year with a spouse	
	Any director or executive of the fund and any knowledgeable employee	

INVESTOR TYPES		
Qualified Clients (QCs)	**Qualified Purchasers (QPs)**	**Qualified Institutional Buyer (QIBs)**
If a person or entity qualifies as a QC, then an RIA can charge them a performance fee	A QP can invest in a fund using the 3c7 exemption of the '40 Act, which can take as many as 2,000 investors	A QIB is allowed to trade privately placed securities with other QIBs with shorter holding periods and no SEC registration
Qualifications	Qualifications	Qualifications
A natural person or company that has at least $1 million under management of the investment adviser	Any natural person who owns $5 million in investments (net of liabilities)	A company or entity that manages at least $100 million in securities on a discretionary basis
or	or	A registered broker/dealer with at least a $10 million investment in non-affiliated securities
A natural person or company that has a net worth of more than $2.1 million	Any family company that owns more than $5 million in investments (net of liabilities)	
or	or	
Any director or executive of the fund and any knowledgeable employee	Any entity that owns at least $25 million in investments (net of liabilities)	
	Any director or executive of the fund and any knowledgeable employee	

Integration

One of the primary purposes of the 3c1 exemption is to keep a fund from being publicly available—hence the reason for the 100-person investor limit. Integration comes into play when a sponsor tries to get around that rule. This typically happens when a sponsor has two substantially similar private funds that he operates with more than 100 investors across both funds. The SEC may determine that the funds are effectively the same fund and consider them as one fund for purposes of the investor count.

While the SEC has not adopted any specific rules or test to determine integration, we can glean some information from some of their no-action letters on the subject.

Oppenheimer Arbitrage Partners LP

In this case, the SEC did not integrate funds because one fund was offered only to tax-exempt investors and the other only to taxable investors. In addition, the version of the tax-exempt fund offering did not engage in short sales or write covered calls like the taxable fund.

Welsh, Carson, Anderson & Stowe

In this case, they were managing institutional funds alongside retail funds, but because they managed them differently in structure and composition, it was allowed. For instance, one fund could use leverage, options and shorting techniques, while the other could not and there was very little overlap in the fund holdings. Also, one fund had a performance fee and the other did not.

Gerald Klein & Associates

The SEC began administrative proceedings against two affiliated advisers at Gerald Klein & Associates because they deemed two funds should be integrated. Both funds had similar investment strategies, but one had the option to allow up to 15% of its assets invested in fixed income securities. Ultimately, the fund portfolios were deemed to be too similar, and were integrated.

Frontier Capital Management Company

Frontier Capital Management Company was refused no-action relief by the SEC for three funds. One fund was to be invested in large cap stocks, the second in small cap stocks and a third in a balanced portfolio of stocks and bonds. The SEC objected due to the fact that all funds had similar investment objectives with potentially overlapping portfolios and ultimately were designed for investors with similar investment profiles.

Using these examples as our guide, we can determine that the following questions are key when determining whether or not a fund will be integrated:

1. Are the funds related in terms of trying to accomplish a common goal?
2. Do the funds share the same sponsor?
3. Will the funds invest in common portfolios?
4. Are the funds offered at about the same time?

5. Are the fees the same or similar in both funds?
6. Are investor profiles for both funds similar?
7. Do the offerings accomplish the same general purpose?
8. Are the sales part of a single plan of financing?
9. Do the sales involve issuance of the same class of securities?
10. Are the sales made at or about the same time?

In addition to considering these questions, there seem to be some general safe harbors that fund sponsors can consider:

1. If there are two funds, one for taxable and one for tax-exempt investors, and there is a substantial difference in investment strategy which would most likely take into consideration the tax-exempt nature of certain investors in the avoidance of unrelated business taxable income (UBTI).
2. The sponsors are different and both entities are unaffiliated.
3. The funds have the same sponsor, but are designed for completely different investor profiles with substantially different portfolio holdings.
4. A 3c1 fund and a 3c7 fund version of the same strategy.

Integration tends to be more of an issue for private funds that invest in public securities and are continuously offered (hedge funds) to new investors. Private equity funds tend to have substantially different portfolios and are closed to new investors. This is why you often see private equity funds with numbered funds 1, 2, 3 and so on, without a concern for integration.

The Consequences of Integration

Integration can have dire consequences. It is vitally important to be cautious and compliant. If the SEC decides that your two or more funds should be integrated, then there are two likely outcomes. These include registering as a mutual fund and/or disgorgement of advisory fees (including performance allocations), and includes paying back interest on those fees to investors. It is not worth it to risk integration.

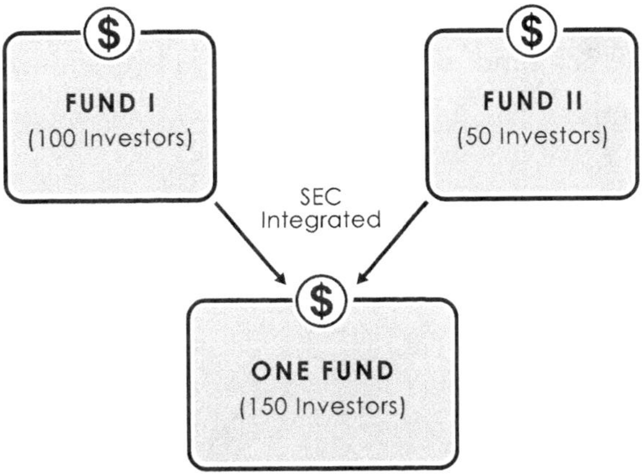

What to Do When You Run Out of Room in a Fund

What do you do when you are closing in on your 100th spot in a 3c1 fund?

One common and safe practice for making more room for investors in a private fund arrangement is to add a 3c7 fund to an already existing 3c1 offering. Here's an example of how it works:

> A fund files an exemption as a 3c1 fund with an accredited investor suitability requirement (Fund A). Fund A subscribes 90 investors. Of those

90 investors, 20 are QPs. The general partner decides that they need to start making more room for future investors, so they create a 3c7 version of the same fund (Fund B) and move the 20 QP investors from Fund A to Fund B. This now gives Fund A 30 investor openings and allows for 1,980 QPs in Fund B.

If the general partner is smart, they will provide for this circumstance in the fund establishment documents so that it is authorized to make the change ahead of time. It is not uncommon for the 3c7 fund to have lower fees to help induce investors to move funds.

What to Do When You Run Out of Investor Spots

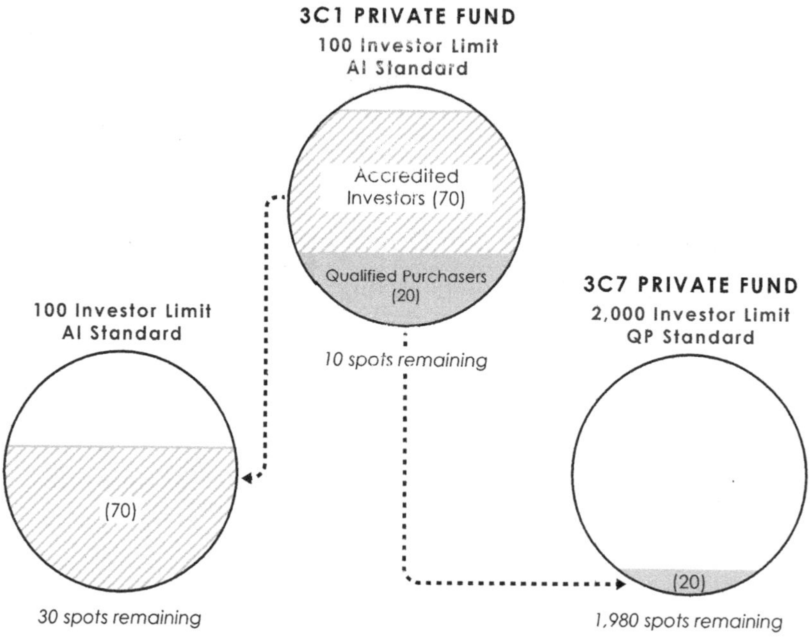

State Exemptions

Up until now, I have addressed the most common exemptions that are available federally. It is important to note that each state has its own rules and exemptions for funds as long as the investors all reside in that state. The variety of rules and regulations are far too many to discuss in this book. At Alta Trust, we choose to use the federal exemptions mentioned earlier: 3c1, 3c5, 3c7 and 3c9. It is safer in the sense that you avoid any potential issues with state nuances and out-of-state investors.

Another consideration for unregistered entities that are advising private funds, even with a federal Reg D exemption and a 3c1 or 3c7 exemption, are any applicable state registration requirements from an investment adviser perspective. This usually comes up when a fund has a high concentration of investors in a single state. Each state varies, but most will have de minimis requirements for registration (e.g., fewer than five clients). Whether a state counts a fund as a single client or looks through to the investors will likely vary by state. It's these types of questions that sponsors need to be aware of and rely on competent legal counsel to guide them in their specific circumstances.

One of the main reasons I started Alta Trust was because the rules and regulations around private funds are something I learned and understand well. I wanted to use my passion to help advisers use them to expand their personal brands. The most important thing I say to our clients when they are thinking about starting a fund and get bogged down in the rules and regs is, "Don't do this alone." I made plenty of mistakes and learned the hard way before my fund strategy was nailed down. Finding the right partner who has been there before makes the whole process easier and protects you from costly mistakes.

Key Points

1. A Reg D Offering refers to a fund offering that is exempt from the '33 Act.
2. Reg D is an SEC regulation that exempt funds must comply with such as: Investor Types, Number of Investors, Offering Solicitation, etc.
3. The most common '40 Act exemptions are 3c1, 3c5 and 3c7.
4. Advisers must be careful to avoid creating funds that can be "integrated".

Exercise:

1. What is the purpose of the '33 Act?
2. What is the purpose of the '40 Act?
3. What are the differences between Accredited Investors, Qualified Clients and Qualified Purchasers?

8

Private Fund Compliance

NOW THAT WE HAVE GONE THROUGH THE RULES AND REGULATIONS at a high level, lets discuss some of the important points when it comes to ensuring proper compliance. We will discuss both adviser compliance and fund compliance. No one likes to talk about rules and regulations, but I like to think about them as the fence around the playground that keeps us safe. We still have plenty of room to play, run and get creative, as long as we know where the fences are and their purpose.

Adviser Compliance

We have talked primarily about registration requirements and exemptions for the fund itself. Now let's focus on the registration of the fund sponsor.

Investment Adviser Registration

The Investment Advisers Act of 1940 (Advisers Act) requires anyone who is "engaged primarily in investing, reinvesting, and trading in securities, and whose own securities are offered to the investing public" and advises more than $100 million in assets must register with the SEC.

An adviser with less than $100 million in assets under management would likely register with a state, unless there is an applicable exemption.

The Exempt Adviser

There is an exception to the SEC adviser registration rule above. It says that any entity that would be deemed an adviser under the definition, that solely advises private funds totaling no more than $150 million in assets is considered an exempt reporting adviser (ERA). In other words, if you manage assets exclusively for one or more private funds with aggregate assets of less than $150 million, you don't have to register with the SEC. When that adviser surpasses $150 million in assets, the firm must register with the SEC.

If you are an adviser reading this, you already know the time and expense that can go into registering as an adviser with the SEC; however, if you are successful enough in your private fund endeavors, it may be unavoidable. Sponsors should also be cognizant of any applicable state registration requirements.

Adviser Performance Fees

One common hallmark of a private fund is the existence of a performance allocation or incentive compensation to the general partner. This comes in the form of the general partner receiving a percentage of the fund's growth as compensation. It is important that RIAs are aware that if they plan to receive any incentive or performance compensation, the fund must meet a higher level of suitability for its investors beyond accredited investor. Rule 205-3 under the Advisers Act allows an adviser to receive client performance fees **only** when the client is considered a qualified client.

Under Rule 205-3, a qualified client is defined as any of the following:

1. The client of an investment adviser who invests at least $1 million with that adviser
2. An individual with $2.1 million in net worth, not including a principal residence
3. An executive, director, trustee or general partner of the investment adviser
4. An employee of the investment adviser who is involved in the investment activities of the adviser

As with an accredited investor, a general partner can accept the investor's representation that they are a qualified client with no additional need to verify, unless they have reason to believe that they do not qualify.

The qualified client requirement as it relates to performance fees only applies to SEC-registered investment advisers and not unregistered entities. State-registered advisers should consult with their own legal counsel to comply with any state-specific regulations.

Charging Performance Fees to Accredited Investors

Entities that are not registered with the SEC as investment advisers can charge accredited investors performance fees with no problem. Oftentimes, a separate non-registered entity is created by the RIA to specifically avoid qualified client standards with respect to charging performance fees. The new entity, which is the general partner, may then choose to engage with the RIA to manage the fund portfolio on behalf of the general partner for a traditional management fee. The performance allocation is remitted to the newly created entity which is the general partner. *(Note: Advisers should work closely with their legal counsel to ensure that the new entity is unique enough to not trigger SEC concerns.)*

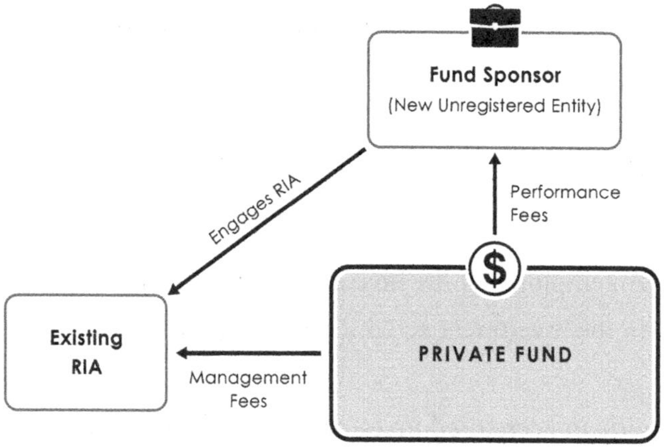

Potential Conflicts of Interest

As an RIA, you are likely very attuned to any possible conflicts of interest between you and your clients. Isn't that one of the main reasons people choose a fee-based adviser over a broker? You want to make sure that you have your client's best interests at the forefront of your recommendations.

If you are an ERISA plan fiduciary, you have a further duty to act in the best interests of your client. I love that this is how investment advisers work, but...

I also appreciate the idea that sophisticated investors, with resources and representation from accountants and attorneys, can make educated decisions whether to make an investment—even if there are some disclosed conflicts. That is one of the beauties of private funds and one of the reasons that only dealing with accredited investors, qualified clients and/or qualified purchasers is critical. It can be okay to have conflicts of interest if you fully disclose them.

Even though it may be okay to have disclosed conflicts, it is not okay to do anything unethical. Double dipping on fees is one of those things that must be avoided. If you are soliciting an investment in a private fund from an advisory client, make sure you don't charge them an advisory fee, and make it clear that you are not "advising" them to invest in your private fund. Your advisory contract (or a side agreement) should specifically carve out the private fund from your advisory agreement, and you should never charge fees on the private fund assets in addition to what you would otherwise earn in your advisory agreement. Some of our clients prefer to charge their advisory fee and choose to create a special share class in the private fund with no fees to the adviser or its affiliates. However you do it, don't charge twice.

Adviser Custody

No adviser wants to take custody, but when it comes to sponsoring a private fund, it has historically come with the territory.

Per the SEC, "An adviser has custody of client assets, and therefore must comply with the rule, when it holds, 'directly or indirectly,' client funds or securities or [has] any authority to obtain possession of them."

According to this definition, a general partner would be deemed to have custody of a fund's assets regardless of whether or not the fund assets are held at a bank or brokerage firm.

But what if the general partner for a hedge fund holds the accounts at a prime broker like Goldman Sachs? Wouldn't Goldman Sachs be the custodian? This is a good point, but the definition also references advisers who have indirect access to the fund assets. Because the general partner will be the one opening up the account on behalf of the fund at Goldman Sachs, they will also have authority to remove the funds, close the account, etc. This certainly meets the requirement of "having authority to obtain possession" of the fund assets.

If an adviser is deemed to have custody, they must meet certain requirements such as:

1. Use a "qualified custodian," which primarily includes banks and broker/dealers among other possibilities;
2. Ensure that quarterly statements be sent to clients;
3. Audit the fund by a PCAOB-registered auditor; and
4. Submit to periodic surprise audits.

One of the ways that advisers can avoid jumping through all of the SEC custody hoops is to ensure that the private fund is audited annually and that the audited financials are distributed to all the investors within 120 days of the fiscal year-end.

With few exceptions, Alta Trust requires every private fund that we serve to have an annual audit. Not only does it help protect the adviser from the SEC custody issues just discussed, but it is reassuring to the investors, the sponsor and all parties involved.

However, we don't stop there when it comes to trying to shield advisers from custody concerns. As we discussed earlier, our business trust structure is particularly appealing to investment adviser sponsors. The Trust Agreement is written such that Alta Trust takes custody of the fund assets and the sponsor is specifically prevented from accessing them. This provides another layer of protection to the adviser and the investors. While it is impossible to know how the SEC will view any given arrangement, the business trust structure provides another layer of protection for the sponsoring adviser.

Finally, advisers should always disclose any private fund that they sponsor or manage in their ADV.

Fund Compliance

It's easy to get excited about all the possibilities of launching a new fund — the excitement of the investors, the investment opportunities awaiting and how potentially lucrative the fund may be for all involved. I am going to interrupt your visions of glory to make sure you are focused on executing on those dreams so they can become a reality.

Fund compliance is an easily overlooked topic. It's not glamorous or exciting, but it is critical to your success. The last thing you want is to expose yourself to undue regulatory scrutiny or litigation, or to create a poor reputation with your client base or within the industry at large. I have seen several private funds that had no business being in business, and I would have trusted my money at the casino before I ever entrusted it with these funds. On the flip side, it only adds to the investor's enthusiasm when they know that their money is in good hands. Every adviser needs to develop a compliance program to make sure that every detail is checked and every item accounted for. For instance, don't worry too much about having to ask your clients to provide certain information such as a driver's license, passport or utility bill prior to investing, or giving them a large Private Offering Memorandum (POM) to review. It shows them that you are serious about what you are doing, which will give them confidence in the way that you will handle their money.

Your Private Fund Compliance Program

Every private fund sponsor needs to have a proactive plan to ensure that their private fund is always properly run and in compliance. Below are a few items that should be accounted for. You can also visit **privatefundsmadesimple.com** for a more detailed compliance checklist.

▶ Federal and State Filings

- **IRS:** Each fund needs its own employer identification number as a filing entity with the IRS. This can be accomplished at **www.irs.gov.**
- **SEC:** For any fund using the Reg D exemption, you must file within 15 days from the date of the first subscription into the fund.

- **Blue Sky State Securities Filings:** Anytime you have an investor subscribe into the fund from a new state of residence or a state where they are the only investor residing, you must make a notification filing on behalf of the fund in that state. State fund filings are often called blue sky filings. You typically have 15 days after the first subscription from someone in that state to file. There is usually a small cost associated with the filing and some filings must be renewed each year.

▶ Know Your Customer

Congratulations, your fund is launched and you have your first investor! Before you subscribe the investor into the fund, you need to perform some investor due diligence. This is called know your customer (KYC), which are checks to ensure that the investor is in fact who they say they are and that they are not laundering any illegal funds. Here are some of the recommended checks we perform at Alta Trust on behalf of our clients. It may seem like a lot, but it will help build confidence with your investors.

1. Verify the investor's residence (e.g., LexisNexis™, utility bill or other documentation).
2. Obtain a passport or driver's license.
3. Obtain a signed W-9 form.
4. Gather contact information — email and mobile phone number (you will need these to ensure secure client communications).
5. Ask for sources of wealth and assets.

6. Confirm political or celebrity status.
7. If the investor is an entity like a trust or corporation, ensure that you have copies of the organization documents.
8. Submit prospective investor information to the Office of Foreign Assets Control (OFAC) of the U.S. Department of the Treasury. They enforce economic and trade sanctions against U.S.-targeted foreign countries, regimes, terrorists, etc. Each investor should be checked against the OFAC list prior to investment.
9. Submit information to the Financial Crimes Enforcement Network (FinCEN), also under the direction of the U.S. Department of Treasury. The mission of FinCEN is to fight against the illicit use of the financial systems in the United States. You should check your prospective investors against the FinCEN list because you want to avoid doing business with anyone on their watch list.
10. Perform a Google search to make sure there is nothing suspicious about your investor.
11. A simple, but effective check is to compare the incoming wire information on the subscription with the information that you have about the investor on file. Wire transfers are also a good way to accept money because the wiring bank also performs their own KYC checks.

Any prospective foreign investors should go through additional verification checks. At Alta Trust, we provide all the above checks on potential investors for our sponsors.

ERISA

The Employee Retirement Income Security Act (ERISA) governs retirement plans and has rules that apply to persons or entities that control the management of a plan or the assets of a plan. It comes into play with private funds when 25% or more of the interests in the fund are held by ERISA-qualified retirement plans or individual retirement accounts as spelled out in a Department of Labor rule called the Plan Asset Regulation. The question then becomes, "What difference does it make if a fund becomes an ERISA fund?"

- The assets of the fund are treated as plan assets, and the fund adviser becomes an ERISA fiduciary and must comply with restrictions on conflicts of interest related to fund assets.
- There are certain limitations with respect to block trades and cross trades. For example, the interests of the plan should not exceed 10% of the block trade.
- Fund documents need to be reviewed for compliance with ERISA requirements. For instance, in a Limited Partnership Agreement, the standard indemnity clause regarding gross negligence of the adviser is not enforceable under ERISA, and liability exculpatory clauses are not permitted at all.
- An ERISA fund manager must acknowledge its fiduciary status under ERISA rules and needs to be in compliance with ERISA requirements at all times.

The 25% threshold is calculated each time there is a change in ownership of equity interest of the fund and does not include any investment by the general partner. The calculation also applies at the class level, which means that if one share class of a fund meets the 25% ERISA threshold, then the entire fund is considered an ERISA fund. (There is an exception built into the Plan Asset Regulation for funds that are "operating companies." An operating company is one that is engaged in the production or sale of a product or service other than the investment of capital or in which at least 50% of the fund assets are held in real estate or venture capital entities where the fund manager has the right to substantially participate directly in the management or development activities of the entities.)

Any pooled vehicles that are invested in the fund must also be scrutinized as to who the beneficial owners are for the pool. This look-through requirement must be considered when calculating the 25% threshold.

Once it is determined that a fund is an ERISA fund, there are also certain prohibited transactions and party-in-interest transactions as defined under Section 406 of ERISA and section 4975 of the Internal Revenue Code (IRC) that need to be considered. For example, performance fees may be considered self-dealing prohibited transactions unless certain requirements are met. Soft dollars represent a problem under ERISA, and there are additional required disclosures to assist plans in filing their annual Form 5500, which must disclose compensation (both direct and indirect) paid to the adviser by the plan.

Cybersecurity, Data Retention and Documentation

According to SEC Rule 204-2, fund data should be archived in an easily accessible location. In this modern era, that usually means the cloud. Further, the rule states that the data should be archived for at least five years and, in some cases, seven years.

Be sure to keep track of all signed documents by the investors, as well as all requests, emails, correspondence, etc. Overdocumentation should be your problem — "if you can't prove it, it didn't happen." Our clients enjoy the benefit of Alta Trust keeping duplicate copies of everything, so that the risk of a documentation gap is significantly less.

Finally, in addition to other considerations, the following should be thought through prior to launch:

- Business Continuity and Disaster Recovery
- SEC and state adviser requirements
- FINRA – particularly as it relates to paying commissions out of the fund
- Commodity Futures Trading Commission (CFTC) – usually applies when trading commodities, futures and currencies
- National Futures Association (NFA)

The Valuation

Your fund may be valued every month, quarter or year. It is important to have some basic checks in place to be reasonably certain about the value of the fund. If you are using an outside administrator to provide valuations, be sure to review them thoroughly. They should provide you a recent SOC1 operational audit that shows an independent auditor has reviewed their internal fund processes and confirms their compliance with those processes.

It is important to check their work when they provide the valuation report. If there is a third-party custodian or third-party fund that is being invested in, make sure the positions and balances reconcile. You should also check the security prices that were used in the valuation to ensure they are accurate. A review of the income and expense accruals is also important. Remember that you are putting your name on the valuation — it is your fund and it represents you, even if someone else is performing the work. Make sure it is correct.

Redemptions / Distributions

Redemptions are allowable by a fund either by way of the offering documents or at the sponsor's discretion. Most venture capital and private equity funds offer limited or no redemption rights to investors during the life of the fund. Hedge funds, on the other hand, typically allow for investors to come in and out of the fund, subject to certain lock-up and notice requirements (gates). Depending on the fund's investment approach, it may provide for scheduled or discretionary distributions of principal and/or income.

A typical hedge fund will have a monthly valuation frequency. An investor can only redeem his shares at the end of a month, assuming they are out of any applicable lock-up period. Frequently, the fund offering documents provide for a notice period such as 30 days. For example, if someone wants to redeem a portion or all of their investment on December 31st, they must notify the general partner by November 30th. This gives the fund time to create the liquidity without harming the remaining investors. The valuation is usually finalized one to two weeks after the month-end, at which time the investor will receive a wire transfer to settle the redemption.

The general partner may determine in their discretion whether or not to honor a redemption request. They may determine that a redemption at that time would adversely impact other investors and then choose to delay the redemption. On the other hand, a general partner may choose to accommodate time-sensitive requests by providing for a special valuation of the fund and allowing an investor to exit earlier than normal if the fund documents permit.

When full redemptions are requested, it is typical for the general partner to withhold 10% of the redemption to allow for any true-ups or adjustments at the end of the year. Once the audit is finalized, the general partner will send any withheld balance, plus or minus any adjustments to the investor.

It is important to have a structured process in place for the payment of redemptions and distributions to the investors. If this is not in place, it could be your single greatest liability. Due to the danger of identity theft, it is imperative that you have strong controls in place (and have a partner like Alta Trust) to ensure that you have verification layers and are sending money to the right person and to the right place.

I recommend gathering the investor's banking information up front on the Subscription Agreement. This makes it easy to check against the incoming subscription wire, which will give you confidence when it comes time to send money out. At Alta trust, it is our practice to only send money according to the same instructions that we received at the beginning, except in rare circumstances.

This is the safest way to handle distributions and redemptions. However, you should have protocols in place to update those banking instructions, when necessary. The following are additional steps you may consider before sending any distributions or redemptions:

1. Signed paperwork (this may include e-signature documents verified through a LexisNexis check or a text to their mobile device)

2. In-person verification call to the number on file

3. Dual internal verifications

The key to redemptions and distributions is to provide flexibility for yourself as the sponsor, so that you don't get stuck in a bad situation where you are required to make a distribution or redemption and you don't have the liquidity. It is smart to have a rigid process that you follow religiously for actually making the payments.

The Audit

Fund audits are technically optional, BUT you should nearly always have an audit. As stated earlier, at Alta Trust we only want to deal with audited funds. The only funds that may reasonably not be audited are friends and family funds and special purpose vehicles, so long as the underlying investment is audited (and even then, you may still want an audit). Barring those exceptions, the fund should have an annual audit performed by a CPA firm with an expertise in fund audits. Having an audited fund will allow you to represent yourself and the fund as legitimate, which will only help your fundraising efforts. It is better for everyone involved to have regular audits performed.

In terms of how the audit works in practice, the general partner will engage the auditor, but the fund's third-party fund administrator, like Alta Trust, will provide most of the audit support. The audit will likely be completed by the end of March on a calendar year-end fund in advance of the partnership filing and distribution of K-1s.

Staying Within the Investment Guidelines

Even though there is usually some latitude in the offering documents, it is still important to keep your promises to investors. An internal or external review should be accomplished periodically and documented to ensure compliance. You may be tempted to invest outside of the fund's investment guidelines, but resist the temptation. The risk is not worth it. If you really feel the need to change something, be sure to take a vote from investors or from a representative group of investors like an "advisory committee" before going forward.

Ultimately, the most effective compliance strategy should have layers. The first layer is an outsourced compliance team, like Alta Trust, who can assist with basic compliance services; a second layer of expert tax and audit specialists; the third layer is the fund's counsel; fourth, a fully outsourced provider may make sense; and finally overseeing and directing it all is the sponsor's compliance team managing all the parties to ensure that everything is working smoothly. Together, these layers come together to create the right formula. They should provide sufficient protection to the adviser, the fund and the investors.

Key Points

1. Advisers need to ensure compliance with the Adviser's Act and state requirements.

2. ERAs do not have to register as advisers with the SEC if they manage less than $150 million of private fund assets.

3. RIAs can only charge performance fees to qualified clients.

4. Avoid ERISA registration if you can by only accepting less than 25% of assets from qualified plans and IRAs.

5. Be careful of taking custody.

6. Take compliance seriously by creating a compliance program and assembling a team.

9

Taxes

AN IMPORTANT CONSIDERATION WHEN LAUNCHING ANY FUND is the taxes. As a sponsor, you need to know what to expect, and your investors also need to have a clear idea of the tax implications of the fund. I will only discuss the most common tax structure here — partnerships.

Partnership Accounting

Limited partnerships are considered partnerships for tax purposes by their very nature. Most limited liability companies and business trusts elect to file as a partnership as well.

Depending on the type of fund you have, the types of investments you make, the number of investors, whether or not you accept in-kind purchases, and other unique aspects of the fund, you may have a pretty straightforward partnership return or one that is complex. I recommend that you not only have a tax expert handle this, but a fund tax expert. Let's discuss a few of the things you need to know.

Partnership Representative

The partnership representative has sole authority to act on behalf of the fund under the partnership audit rules. The partnership representative is usually an employee or owner of the general partnership. When investors agree to invest in a fund, they give up the ability to represent themselves individually with respect to the fund and grant that authority to the fund's partnership representative who represents the fund and investors collectively in dealings with the IRS. The partnership representative also has the authority to make binding tax-related decisions for the fund and its investors.

The Partnership Return and K-1s

The fund must file a partnership return each fiscal year (Form 1065). The 1065 return is informational, and each investor will receive their pro rata share of the income, gains, deductions, etc., as reported on Schedule K-1. The general partner should engage a professional tax firm to prepare the partnership return and K-1s on behalf of the fund.

Sometimes advisers are reluctant to start a private fund because they are worried about issuing K-1s to their investors. The reality is that most accredited investors are accustomed to receiving K-1s and adding one more to the mix is not a big deal. Judging by the feedback we have received from our clients, the concern usually doesn't manifest as a real issue. In any event, good communication with the investor and setting proper expectations will go a long way.

Form 1065 is due two and one-half months after the fund's fiscal year-end before extensions and can be extended until eight and one-half months after year-end. Most partnerships use calendar year-ends because their owners also use calendar year-ends for their personal returns. K-1s are generally issued to investors in March to give them time to file their personal returns before April 15th. While most accredited investors file extensions anyway, by giving your investors their K-1s in March, at least you won't be the reason they extend.

There are certain types of funds, like fund of funds, that may need to be extended because they must first obtain information from underlying partnerships before they can file the partnership return. It is important to let investors know if you expect to have investments that may cause a delay in providing them information for their tax returns.

Your fund may also require state tax returns. The requirements vary by state, but may be based upon the location of the adviser, the location of any business activities of the fund or the residency of some of the investors in the fund.

Tax Allocations

As an example, if a partnership has two equal partners and has $100,000 of taxable income and economic income in a year, how is this split? If you guessed $50,000 is allocated to each, you would be half right. Each partner would have economic income equal to 50% of the overall income for the year. However, the allocation of taxable income may differ, based upon the specifics of when each partner owned an interest in the partnership.

Let's look at an example of a fund with only one asset. Partner A was a partner when an asset was purchased for $10,000 and it appreciated to $60,000 before Partner B became a 50% partner. Partner B contributed $60,000 at the beginning of the year that did not earn income while the asset appreciated to $160,000 of value. The partnership sold some of the stock to generate $100,000 of taxable capital gains.

Both Partner A and Partner B should split the $100,000 of economic income, and each partner would have a capital account of $110,000 at the end of the year reflecting the beginning balance of $60,000 each and their share of the increase in value during the year ($50,000 each). However, would it be fair to split the taxable gain equally? Likely not. As Partner A really held the partnership when the assets had economic, but not taxable income, the tax law would generally cause more of the taxable gain to be allocated to Partner A.

The specifics of these tax allocation rules can get very complicated, and you may hear a variety of phrases like "lot layering," "aggregation with full netting" and "aggregation with partial netting," which all are intended to solve these problems. The basic concept is that the tax rules cause each investor to ultimately recognize taxable gains based on the unrealized gains that investors earned while owning the fund. In addition, funds often implement a process known as "stuffing," which is an allocation of tax gains or losses to a particular investor upon a full or partial redemption of their interest in the funds.

Your tax adviser should walk you through these challenging rules and determine the best approach for your fund.

Tax Lots

Tax laws allow a partnership to specifically identify the lot of the security that is being sold. In order to use this specific identification, which may be used for specific tax planning purposes, you must notify the broker at the time of the sale (i.e., selling lots with the highest cost basis to minimize taxable gain). However, most brokers will require a standing default tax lot relief method to be used for those times when you don't identify which lot is being sold. The most common of these methods are high cost and first in, first out (FIFO).

Tax Liabilities

It is important for investors to be aware that depending on the investment approach, certain funds may generate a tax liability shown on an investor's K-1, but not generate any income or returns in order to pay for it. In this case, the investor must pay the tax liability from another source or may request a withdrawal of capital from the fund to pay the taxes. Many funds will make a tax distribution, if possible, to help investors pay the taxes generated from the investment in the fund.

Trader Fund vs. Investor Fund

A determination is made each year as to whether a fund is a trader fund or an investor fund. The determination is made by the sponsor after considering the purpose and activity of the fund. The test for this is admittedly a gray one, but essentially if a fund makes investments and holds on to them for longer periods of time, it would not qualify as a trader fund. However, if a fund has a high turnover and investments are made and exited over short periods of time, then the fund would likely qualify as a trader fund. A trader fund generally looks at short-term market swings, where an investor fund generally focuses on longer-term returns.

The impact of trader versus investor status for a fund relates to how expenses of the fund are treated by individual investors of the fund. Specifically, trader funds are deemed to be in a trade or business for tax purposes and the expenses are deductible as business expenses. An investor fund incurs investment expenses which are not deductible by individual partners. Taxation as a trader fund has tax benefits, but the classification must have economic reality.

The Performance Allocation (Carried Interest)

In addition to management fees, many funds have an incentive allocation in which the fund distributes a portion of the fund's profits to the general partner. A common split is a 20% performance allocation to the general partner, in which case 20% of all the income or capital gains earned by the fund (or a particular investor) will be allocated to the general partner on an annual basis. For example, if a fund returned $100 of unrealized gain before incentive allocation, $20 of this unrealized gain would be allocated to the general partner.

There are specific "carried interest" rules that may cause some capital gains allocated to the general partner on positions held by the fund less than three years to be treated as short-term capital gain instead of long-term capital gain. Make sure your tax preparer is well equipped to handle these complications!

Separate Accounts vs. Funds

There may be significant advantages to setting up a fund if an adviser charges a performance fee on separately managed accounts. Performance fees charged to a client who is an individual taxpayer in a separate account are **never** deductible by the client. In addition, you as the adviser, would treat the performance fee as income taxable at ordinary income rates and may be subject to self-employment income tax.

Setting up a fund for your managed account investors, even a fund for just a single investor, and converting this performance fee to a performance allocation may be a tax win-win for your investors and yourself. If structured correctly, you may even be able to contribute the client's existing holdings in their accounts into a fund on a tax-free basis to help get your fund going.

Example: Performance Fee in a Separately Managed Account Versus a Private Fund

Facts: An individual investor earns $500,000 of long-term capital gains and the adviser charges a 20% incentive.

- Managed Account Treatment of Performance Fee
    - Investor has $500,000 of capital gains and has $100,000 (the performance allocation) of nondeductible investment expenses.
    - Adviser receives $100,000 of advisory fee income, taxable as ordinary income.
    - The result is the investor and adviser collectively have $600,000 of taxable income ($500,000 of capital gain to the investor and $100,000 of ordinary income to the adviser) on the $500,000 of economic income.
- Fund Treatment as an Allocation of Profits
    - Investor has $500,000 of long-term capital gains before an incentive allocation. The performance allocation dictates that the general partner receives $100,000 of the capital gains. This results in a net $400,000 of capital gain recognized by the investor.
    - The general partner is allocated $100,000 of capital gains income from the fund. The character of this gain as either long-term or short-term capital gain will depend on the carried interest rules.
    - Accordingly, the investor and general partner recognize a total of $500,000 of capital gains if the incentive amount is structured as an allocation of partnership income.

Unrelated Business Income Tax (UBIT)

UBIT is a tax paid by tax-exempt entities on certain types of income. The tax rate on UBIT is the U.S. corporate tax rate.

Tax-exempt entities include:

- IRAs
- Pensions
- Endowments
- Foundations
- Charities and other Section 501(c)(3) organizations

UBIT is only paid by tax-exempt entities on unrelated business income tax. Most forms of portfolio income, such as dividends, interest income and capital gains from the sale or exchange of capital assets, are not treated as UBIT. However, income from "debt financed property" is considered to be UBIT. So, funds that use margin or borrow may generate UBIT for its tax-exempt investors. There are some exceptions to this borrowing rule, such as the use of loans for short-term administrative convenience or to fund redemption requests. Options and short sales normally do not trigger UBIT either.

In addition to trading funds that use margin, real estate and oil and gas investments are often debt-financed and may generate UBIT. In addition, private equity investments in operating partnerships or investments in Master Limited Partnerships (MLPs) often generate UBIT.

In order to avoid UBIT, a tax-exempt investor such as a pension plan or endowment may prefer to invest in an offshore fund in order to block the UBIT. With an offshore fund, typically set up in a low- or no-tax foreign country, there may be other tax consequences such as dividend tax withholding. A tax-exempt investor will want to consider all tax ramifications before making an investment in an offshore fund.

Other Tax Considerations

There are so many other topics that could be covered in this chapter. The following are a few issues that I have worked with our tax adviser partners to address with fund managers:

- In-kind contributions of securities to funds
- In-kind distributions of securities to redeeming partners
- Various tax elections that may be available (e.g., mark to market election for traders)
- Tax rules of specific derivative investments held by funds
- Impact of wash sale, straddle and constructive sales rules
- Rules specific to investing in debt instruments
- Real estate holdings in a fund
- State and local tax filings
- Use of offshore funds
- Tax reporting of foreign investments
- Fund of funds

Several books have been written about the tax complexities of private funds. I highly recommend working with a tax adviser specializing in private fund issues. This allows fund managers to focus on what they do best — manage investments for their clients, knowing that these complexities are adequately addressed.

Key Points

1. Be sure to work with a qualified auditor and tax adviser with significant fund experience.
2. Before you launch a private fund, consider the tax implications to you as the general partner and to the investors — and set the proper expectations in the offering documents.
3. If you are charging or plan to charge a "performance fee," always do it in a fund as a "performance allocation."
4. If you are targeting pensions, endowments or other tax-exempt investors, avoid UBIT (or provide some relief from UBIT, perhaps through an offshore feeder fund).

10

Raising Capital

WE'VE GOTTEN THROUGH THE HEAVY STUFF. NOW IT'S TIME TO look ahead to when the private fund is legally up and running and needs capital to begin employing its investment strategy and benefiting your investors. There are a few different ways to approach capital raising. However, before we start on each of the approaches, we need to be clear on the pitch. If you don't have your pitch down, it won't matter who you talk to or how good your offering is if "the why" isn't obvious to the prospective investor.

The Pitch

The first thing to know is that having a compelling investment strategy on its own does not guarantee that anyone will be interested in your fund. Great stories get funded before great strategies. When you have both, you are primed for success if you are willing to put in the work—and it will likely be work. Don't be nervous. The work will pay off, but you should go into this with the proper expectation that it will take some serious effort on your part to get the fund off the ground. It becomes easier after you have a successful fund on the books. Even though past performance is no guarantee of future results, it certainly provides some comfort to investors.

Crafting the Right Story

Remember, great stories get funded before great strategies. The key to raising capital is to create a story that resonates with your target investor. It should include all the facts, but also generate emotion and captivate the investor's attention. Human beings' brains are wired to connect with stories, even the most sophisticated investors. I like to follow the simple format from the book *Building a StoryBrand,* by Donald Miller. Donald Miller goes through the elements of storytelling and how every effective story follows the same pattern. I recommend the book but will summarize the elements here.

▶ 1. The Villain

Good stories start with a villain. The villain will be whatever problem your fund proposes to solve. If your fund makes investments that are good for the environment, then pollution might be your villain. If the fund brings affordable products to the masses, then a big corporate bully that gets in the way might be your villain. Dating websites fight against loneliness. Assisted living centers fight against a poor quality of life for the elderly. Making a fund available to people who didn't know they could invest in something interesting and exclusive might be fighting the battle for leveling the playing field. A biotech fund may invest in companies trying to find a breakthrough against a medical disease. Think hard about what problem you are really trying to solve and make it as real and vivid as possible when you present to investors.

▶ 2. The Hero

Now that we have a villain or a problem, we need a hero with a solution. Advisers are always tempted to place themselves in the hero role. In reality, pitches work best when the investor is positioned as the hero. We all wake up in the morning wanting to write our own story rather than have someone else write it for us. We want to be the hero who can swoop in to save the day and help right the wrongs of the villain. Your heroes, the investors, need to believe in the villain your fund is fighting. They need to want to solve the problems caused by the villain. Your fund needs to have the power to actually right the wrongs and solve these problems. You must portray your fund as THE solution to the problem the villain causes. Of course, everything needs to be accurate and honest, so if your fund doesn't truly help solve the problem or vanquish the villain, you may need to change your villain. Remember that investors don't invest in the best business plans, they invest in the best stories.

▶ 3. The Guide

In the book *Building a Story Brand*, Donald Miller reminds us that every good story has a guide—like Yoda for Luke Skywalker. In this case, you are the guide. As you share your pitch as a story, you help the investors see why you are the right person to guide their investment to success. The plan you present to them, your private fund, is a pathway to help them achieve their goals and conquer the villain all at the same time.

4. The Happy Ever After

Finally, you must help your investors visualize life after this fight between good and evil. Your pitch should emphasize all the good that will be accomplished by the fund. Depending on the investment strategy, the noble benefits could be the new affordable housing that will be created, the high paying jobs that the fund will generate or maybe the new technology that will allow equal access to financial products. As you round out the benefits, you will of course include the potential financial return as the prize. It should be obvious to the prospective investor that your fund will leave a permanent mark on them and the world — in a good way.

Most advisers are a little leery about over promising and perhaps saying too much, and for good reason. I would caution you to not oversell or undersell your fund strategy. There will be disclosures in the marketing materials and private offering memorandum, telling investors about the risks and that there are no guarantees. So, go for the pitch. Pitch it confidently, proudly and realistically!

Here are some short, fictional examples of how the elements above can build into a clear, compelling pitch.

> Everyone deserves access to quality health care. But many Americans simply can't afford it. You want to help, but aren't sure how to approach a problem as big as health care. We understand. We believe we can start making small improvements in the healthcare system by investing in proven tools and new

> ventures that help fellow Americans gain access to the health care they deserve. Our fund will give more Americans access to quality health care and will give our investors a healthy return. By pooling our resources, we can make a difference while still working toward your investment goals. Isn't it time to invest in something that will make a difference in the lives of our fellow Americans?

> Awesomeville is made great by the people who call it home. Yet outside investors are making investments that are changing the fabric of this town we love. You don't want outsiders to determine the future of Awesomeville. Neither do we. We believe our community should receive investments from the people like us who call it home, not outside investors. By banding together as neighbors, we can invest in public and private opportunities and keep our community strong. Our fund is only open to people like you who live and work here. Not only will we invest in Awesomeville, we will create returns for our investors as well. Those returns will also help our community become stronger. Isn't it time we set the course for Awesomeville's future?

Now that we have the story structure down, let's look to the nuts and bolts of the pitch.

Budgets

Every sophisticated investor will assume that you think your budget is conservative. They have heard it all before. It is important that you take some time to give them comfort around your abilities to budget, as well as the context and assumptions you have made, so they can judge for themselves whether the budget is conservative or realistic.

Projections

Projections are important to share, but be careful about how "pie in the sky" they are. Investors will likely discount your projections mentally and may discount your pitch altogether if the projections are not in the realm of possibility. Remember, whether they believe that your fund will invest in the next Facebook or not is irrelevant. None of the original Facebook investors could have likely dreamed of their current success.

What is important is that you show them a likely path to a healthy return. "Realistic" is in the eye of the beholder. Provide projections that you can support with as much data as possible. If you return anything beyond that, no one will complain. *(Note: I recommend providing high level projections at the beginning, with the detailed backup on hand if they ask more specific questions.)*

Competition

If you don't address competition in your pitch, your prospective investors will likely think that you are just another dreamer with your head in the clouds. Address your competition in a forthright and thoughtful way with good answers to obvious questions like:

- "Why are you a better investment than others?"
- "How easy is it for new competitors to jump into the market?"
- "How easy is it for clients to switch to a competitor?"
- "What advantage do you have over others or vice versa?"

Your Unfair Advantage

For someone to invest, there must be something special about your offering that other people don't offer or that would be very difficult and time-consuming for them to obtain. For instance, you might have a special piece of software, an option on a piece of property, an agreement to bring in a high-profile individual to the deal, a government contract or approval, or an endorsement arrangement. You need to highlight your unfair advantage and make sure they know that you are the only one who can give it to them. If you cannot differentiate, you cannot sell!

Backup

If you aren't prepared to back up each statement you make with facts or credible assumptions, then you likely won't get far. In fact, don't wait to be asked; bring up the data and the support for your assumptions in your pitch. Remember, you are showing them a problem with a solution, and you need to build credibility in the eyes of the investors so they feel like your firm is the right group to guide them and their investment on that journey.

Some ideas for support include:

- **Data:** It's always a good idea to use data to support your position. Use reputable sources such as industry associations, governments and reputable data vendors. Don't ignore opposing data to your thesis either. If you can show it and rebut it in your presentation, you will create significant credibility.

- **Studies:** Depending on what you are pitching, it is always helpful to have reputable studies on your side. For example, if you are pitching a biotech fund, be sure to use articles from medical journals or studies showing the importance of your fund. Just remember to use reputable sources and never distort the findings.
- **Articles and Books:** If the problem that you are helping to solve is truly pervasive and as large as you believe, then there will likely be plenty of articles and current books you can cite to help make your point. You can show credibility by referencing and producing these in your pitch. Remember, most of your investors will want to believe you, but you need to add other voices to your own so that it is a chorus telling your clients that they need to be a part of your fund.

What Your Pitch Should Include:

▶ One-Pager

You may want a one-pager to pique the interest of your potential investors. A one-page illustration highlights, but doesn't go into the details of how you will accomplish your plan — especially anything confidential. The purpose of the one-pager is to garner initial interest without having to give your full pitch to every potential investor. Caution: One potential downside of the one pager is that people may make a quick judgment and screen you out early without hearing the whole pitch.

▶ Non-Disclosure Agreement (NDA)

Depending on the type of fund you are launching and the sensitive nature of your intellectual property, you may want to have a Non-Disclosure Agreement (NDA) ready for those prospective investors who are interested in taking the next step.

▶ Full Presentation (Pitch Deck)

The full presentation should be complete, but as succinct as possible. I recommend about 15 slides or pages, depending on how you plan to present. The pitch deck should cover everything that we discussed previously — telling the story of the villain (the problem), hero (the investor), guide (your solution) and the happy ever after (great returns). Include your unfair advantage, competition and the data to back up all your assumptions. Pack it in, make it really punchy and enticing and remember that you should be able to deliver it completely in less than 20 minutes.

▶ Leave-Behind

This is a synopsis of your pitch that you can leave with your prospective investors, so they will remember your points and lean on the information in order to communicate your pitch to their partners, spouses, or other decision makers or influencers who may need to sign off on the investment. I also recommend that you include the supporting data that you referenced in your pitch, so they can review it on their own time. A virtual data room is a great substitute for a hard copy leave-behind. And finally, don't forget to keep your materials updated. There is nothing worse than pitching today's investor with last year's information.

Offering Documents

The offering documents include your Limited Partnership Agreement or Trust Agreement, the Private Offering Memorandum and the Subscription Agreement. When a prospect is serious about investing and wants to enter the diligence stage, you will need to make sure the offering documents are readily available.

Additional Confidence-Builders

It's smart for advisers to include in their virtual data room some additional documents that provide peace of mind to investors and show that you have left nothing to chance. It will impress them and give them an indication of the type of firm they are going to do business with and how their investment will be handled. Here are some examples of things you can showcase that will give your investors confidence in your fund's operations:

- Certificate of Trust or Limited Partnership Registration
- Fund Administration Agreement
- Fund Investment Management Agreement
- Bad Actor Certification
- Trustee Charter and Certificate of Good Standing (for business trusts)
- Errors and Omissions Insurance Certificate
- Awards
- News and magazine articles
- Auditor information including credentials and awards

- Attorney information and qualifications
- A video with team members, biographies or information on the fund

Overwhelm your prospective investor with evidence and reassurance that their investment will be in good hands.

▶ What Your Pitch Should Not Include:

- More than 20 slides (keep it under 20 minutes)
- Too much data (although have supplemental data ready)
- Uncertainty
- Anything that would detract from the excitement of the story

Now that you have your pitch, you are almost ready to get out there and start presenting it. Make sure that you practice giving it before you meet with a prospective investor. Consider practicing your pitch with a friend or coworker to make sure that you have it down. Be sure to think of any questions your investor may have and be ready with answers.

Making the Pitch

Anchor Investors

One of the best ways to launch a fund is to launch it with an anchor investor already in place. Ideally, this person or entity is well known and provides credibility to the fund, making it easier for others to invest. Anchor investors often know their value and will require favorable investment terms, but they will make it a lot easier for you to raise capital from other investors.

Advisory Clients

The most obvious place to find investors is within your own high-net-worth client base. You know their history and their situation, likes and dislikes, so it won't be difficult to discuss a new investment opportunity with them. Just make sure you stay out of trouble and don't double charge them!

Institutional Investors (Pensions, Family Offices, Foundations, Endowments, etc.)

Institutional investors are a great place to look for funding. They have constant streams of income to invest and reinvest, and they are comfortable with private fund structures. They typically have structured processes and committees to review investments, so it is essential that you have your pitch buttoned up and looking professional. You can also find these types of investors through databases such as Prequin and Pitchbook.

In-House Sales Team

Some firms take the approach of wholesaling a fund with an internal sales team. The general rule here is that you can pay your employees a commission for bringing investors into a fund, as long as the employees have other duties that are ongoing in nature to the fund and they are not solely salespeople. If you do have individuals who are strictly in a sales role, they must be registered with a broker/dealer to receive a commission. Check with your securities counsel on your specific situation.

Placement Agents

In order to get paid out of a private fund for distribution, you must either be the sponsor or you must be a registered broker/dealer. If you are the sponsor of a fund, you have the option of paying an offering agent to help you raise money. They will likely charge approximately 2% of the capital raised for real estate and private equity or some split of your general partner fees.

Selling Through Other Investment Advisers

Working with other advisers can be a great way to raise assets in a fund. You will need a strong value proposition to help them see the value of the fund for their clients. They may recommend that their clients invest directly into the fund or they can always create a feeder fund structure of their own. This can work well in certain instances. The following is a real life example of a feeder fund structure we put in place.

Goldenrod Example

Goldenrod is a registered investment adviser that focuses on real estate investments in the central United States. Goldenrod historically raised capital through personal relationships, large family offices and corporate investments. Attempting to raise capital more efficiently, Goldenrod decided that with the launch of their third fund, they would take investments from other RIAs, who may want to create a feeder fund that would invest in the third Goldenrod fund. Goldenrod approached Alta Trust about creating a feeder structure for their third private fund. Here's how it works:

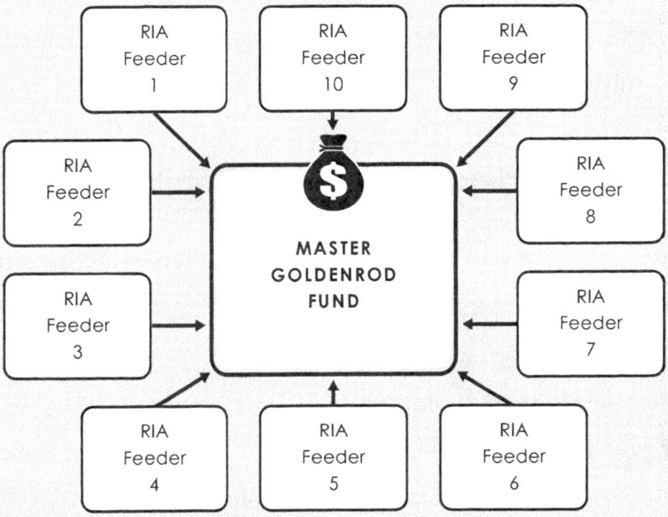

We worked with Goldenrod to create template documents to use with the RIAs so that we could launch funds at a very low cost. Both the launch and the ongoing administration we offer are very turnkey, which helped the RIAs feel comfortable taking this on.

What are the benefits of an approach like this?

1. Goldenrod can work directly with the RIAs and avoid working directly with the RIA's clients.
2. The RIA clients can invest smaller amounts instead of each investor having to meet the $5 million minimum investment on their own.

3. The RIA can offer something truly unique and branded to their clients.
4. The RIA can offer the feeder fund to clients (at no additional cost) and to non-clients for a fee.
5. This approach leverages the magic of exclusivity that was discussed earlier.

Some Final Advice on Raising Capital

Regardless of how you decide to raise capital, remember that it may be more work than you think, especially if you go outside your own client base. Plan to make your pitch to many potential investors to get the assets you are looking for.

If you feel uneasy about a potential investor, then pass. The situation would likely create more problems for you than the investment is worth.

The worst thing you can do is come across desperate or needy when you are pitching your fund. Make sure that you are pitching from a position of strength. Your prospects will sense it if you are unsure and they will instinctively retreat. Remember, there is a lot of money out there, but you are the only one with your deal.

When You Get a "Yes"

Always ask investors that say "yes" follow-up questions such as, "Of all that I presented, what was the most compelling reason for you to invest?" You want to know what is resonating or not with investors, so you can adjust your future pitches. Make sure to ask them if they know others who may want to invest.

When You Get a "No"

You may not have received a commitment, but don't leave empty-handed. At the very least, you can collect information that will help you in the future. You could say something like, "What was it that kept you from investing today?" or "Thank you for your time. I understand that this fund may not be a good fit for you, but do you know someone who might be interested?" or "I understand that my fund wasn't a good fit for you. What kind of investment are you looking for?" Ideally, you will leave on good terms with a correct idea of the types of investments they want and a name or two of investors who might be interested. Better yet, if they do give you a name of a potential investor, ask them to provide a warm email introduction.

Finalizing the Deal

The most important rule of raising capital is this. **The deal is never done until you get the wire.** You can march a prospective client right down the field and think you have made the deal, but that last yard is the hardest. Don't become complacent or take anything for granted. You are allowed to celebrate—but only when the wire hits.

Raising capital gets easier with experience. We have seen many of our advisers struggling with their pitches, even though their offering was strong. So, we have created a program to write their pitches to help improve their fundraising success. If raising capital feels daunting, consider finding a partner you can trust who can help you craft a compelling pitch so you can celebrate finalizing the deal!

Key Points

1. Your pitch should be a story with a villain and a hero.
2. Raising capital requires effort (mostly before you even speak to a potential investor).
3. Consider partnering with other RIAs.
4. There are many ways to raise capital, but clients are usually the best source for investment advisers.
5. Ask follow-up questions when they say "yes" and "no."
6. The deal is never final until the wire transfer comes in!
7. Do you need help getting your pitch just right? Alta Trust can help.

11

The Mistakes Advisers Make and How to Avoid Them

WHEN YOU WORK PRIMARILY WITH INVESTMENT ADVISERS, you begin to hear the same or similar questions quite often. The purpose of this chapter is to answer those questions and help you avoid the pitfalls common to investment advisers.

Can I Treat a Private Fund Like a Mutual Fund?

We talk to many advisers who look at creating a private fund as a way to work around the mutual fund regulations, which admittedly are substantial. While I don't blame them for wanting to find a legal solution to their problem, it is important to understand that private funds are most certainly **not mutual funds.** Don't set up a private fund that really should be a mutual fund.

Can I Get Daily Values?

We are asked from time to time to provide daily values for a private fund because that is what their clients are "used to." Our answer is always that they need to get "used to" a different way or they shouldn't be investing in private funds.

Private fund subscriptions and redemptions are processed manually and not through an automated system like the National Securities Clearing Corporation (NSCC) where mutual funds trade and settle. Private funds also commonly have limited redemption rights, meaning that investors may not be able to easily get out of a fund once they have subscribed. If investors were allowed to come in and out of a fund, tracking the performance allocations would be a nightmare. It is just too complicated and not worth it. The investor needs to be educated appropriately, and it gives the sponsor more room to put the assets to work without interruption. Remember, hedge funds are usually valued monthly and private equity funds and real estate funds are typically valued quarterly.

Can I Sign for Investors?

This is a question that comes up regularly. Advisers are used to clicking a few buttons or sending off files for execution on behalf of their clients. That's how they buy mutual funds for their client accounts, right? That's not how it works with private funds. And the answer is, "No, you cannot sign for a client, unless you have a valid power of attorney." There is no upside to taking on that liability.

Do you really want to be in a position to get sued if an investment goes south and they claim they never wanted it in the first place? This one is easy to avoid. Never do it!

Can I Put My Private Fund on Other Platforms?

Platforms such as Charles Schwab, Fidelity, Pershing, Envestnet and others will sometimes allow private funds to be reflected on the client statements alongside other holdings. This can be a convenient way for investors to view all their holdings in one place. Approval by the platform is required. The requirements typically are as follows:

- POM review
- Subscription Agreement review
- Copy of most recent audit (or signed audit engagement letter for a new fund)
- Auditor must usually be registered with the Public Company Accounting Oversight Board (PCAOB)
- Adviser's Form ADV Part 2

Approval is not always granted and depending on the situation, it may become costly to implement.

How Do Third-Party Advisers Get Paid?

One question that I hear fairly frequently is how a fee-based adviser can get paid in a private fund situation. It is important that investment advisers act in the best interests of their clients and that the clients understand their role. Fee-based advisers would never sell a client A, B or C shares of a mutual fund and receive a commission. They would also never sell their clients anything that would pay them a 12b-1 fee or a trail, which is also considered a commission. The same thinking applies to private funds. Fee-based advisers cannot receive compensation from a fund they don't manage. The following are ways for an adviser to get paid:

▶ Charge a Different Account

The most straightforward way for an adviser to get paid on a private fund they recommend is for the adviser to charge the fee to a different client account. The advisory fee will be calculated on the private fund assets and then the amount is billed to the client's separate account portfolio. Just be sure that the private funds are covered under your advisory agreement with the client and that the arrangement is clear.

▶ Standing Instructions to Liquidate

This method only works with relatively liquid funds (e.g., monthly), but it can be very convenient and effective in the right circumstance. The adviser, the sponsor and the investor in the fund all execute an additional document authorizing the sponsor to liquidate sufficient interests in the fund to pay the adviser. The sponsor is at the same time instructed to remit the fee to the adviser, as outlined in the agreement.

▶ The Feeder Fund Approach

An adviser may want to create their own feeder fund that invests in a master fund, in which case they can charge a management fee in the feeder fund.

Can a Private Fund Be a Qualified Purchaser?

We get this question often. Remember, a 3c7 fund requires investors who have $5 million of investible assets as individuals or $25 million for institutions or entities.

The idea is that a 3c1 fund for accredited investors raises over $25 million. Because the fund has over $25 million in investible assets, some advisers make the argument that they should be able to invest the 3c1 fund assets into a 3c7 fund as a fund investment. Is that possible?

It's a nice idea and would certainly create a good story to potential investors, but it doesn't work. The SEC has said:

> "The statutory definition of qualified purchaser specifies that a trust that is a qualified purchaser must not have been formed 'for the specific purpose of acquiring the securities offered.' The rule makes the same condition applicable to any other company that is a prospective qualified purchaser (whether a family company or another type of company), unless each beneficial owner of the company's securities is a qualified purchaser. The rule thus limits the possibility that a company will be able to do indirectly what it is prohibited from doing directly (i.e., organize a 'qualified purchaser'

entity for the purpose of making an investment in a particular Section 3(c)(7) fund available to investors that themselves did not meet the definition of qualified purchaser)."

The basic premise of the SEC's comments is to disallow investors into any type of investment directly or indirectly for something that they cannot otherwise qualify for on their own.

General Words of Private Fund Wisdom

Start Small

For most advisers, it will make sense to start out small. This could mean a fund that is smaller in size or one that is less complicated to manage, or both. It's best to take the crawl, walk, run approach if you are new to the space. There is a lot you will learn on your first fund and as your expertise grows, so will your value to your investors.

I mentioned earlier the two oil and gas funds that I launched with partners. A year after our first fund launched, we launched our second fund. The second fund was significantly easier to launch and manage and yielded a much greater financial return to our investors than the first one. Our knowledge and understanding grew exponentially after having made both good and bad decisions with our first private fund. Easier and more profitable — sounds good, right?

Don't Be Too Cheap

When you are establishing and running a private fund, it is far less expensive in the long run to hire expertise at the beginning.

You might be thinking to yourself, "How hard can it be?" Unless you have been running private offerings for many years, there is always more to learn and you need experts to keep you and your investors safe.

At Alta Trust, we use excellent legal counsel and insist that all the funds we serve use their own competent legal counsel and a high-quality auditor. We like to use Cohen & Company for most of our private fund audits. Their advice will save you and your investors a lot of money, not to mention all the headaches you will avoid.

A good third-party administrator and compliance team will also make a world of difference. They will provide practical expertise and do all the heavy lifting to make sure your fund is administered properly. At Alta Trust, we have the privilege of working with very smart and accomplished investment advisers—all with very cool investment approaches, many of whom have no idea about how to run a private fund. Keeping their funds running smoothly is a rewarding part of our job.

You are starting small with your first fund and you don't want to overpay—I get it. But don't be too cheap. You want to make sure you are establishing a solid team around your fund. If you do it right, it will show in your fundraising and pay off in the long run.

Accumulate a Track Record

Another benefit of starting small is that it affords you the opportunity to generate a track record. We always say in our industry that past performance does not guarantee future results, but it is a lot easier for an investor to decide to invest if there is some history they can evaluate. In some cases, it may make sense to have an incubator fund with only general partner money to create a track record before you take the fund to outside investors.

Private funds are a great solution for most advisory firms that have over $250 million in assets. If that is you, then it is time to take a hard look at private funds. Get into the space the smart way. Once you do, you will be surprised how many opportunities you begin to see around you!

Don't Accept Non-Accredited Investors

We are often asked about making a private offering available to non-accredited investors. Legally, it is possible to allow up to 35 investors into a 3c1 fund; however, it comes with a substantial additional disclosure requirement and a significant amount of risk. We tell advisers that it is just not worth it. It tends to be small amounts of money for a lot more risk.

Generally, regulators and courts aren't too concerned with wealthy people and institutions taking risks and potentially losing their money, but they like to stand up for the small-time investor. It's advisable to keep private offerings centered on the problem you are trying to solve and avoid confusing the issue. Don't muddy the water with non-accredited investors—keep them invested in mutual funds and ETFs.

✗ **NON-ACCREDITED INVESTORS = MUTUAL FUNDS**

$

✓ **ACCREDITED INVESTORS = PRIVATE FUNDS**

Communicate With Investors

It's impossible to overstate the importance of investor communication. I have personally made the mistake of assuming my investors were fine and letting too much time lapse without an update. If you make that mistake, your investors will not assume "no news is good news." On the contrary, they will begin to worry and assume that things aren't going well, and possibly even think that you are hiding something. Remember, these investments are not public, and investors only receive the information you provide them.

By following these simple suggestions, you and your fund will be off to a great start. Learn from my mistakes and focus on launching your fund the right way.

Key Points

1. Don't treat a private fund like a mutual fund.
2. There are a variety of ways to market a fund to other RIAs, which allows them to get paid.
3. Don't be too cheap.
4. Don't allow non-accredited investors into your private fund.
5. Stay in touch with your investors.

12

Creating Your Own Private Fund

HOPEFULLY BY NOW YOU ARE EXCITED ABOUT THE POSSIBILITIES for both you and your clients. It is time to start putting all the pieces together and building your own private fund. You will likely be surprised at how many different items you need to consider to get it right.

Unfortunately, when we started our first fund, we didn't know a lot of things and the attorney we used was great, but not a specialist. It all worked out in the end, but it would have been nice to have had a better understanding of the options.

Let's go through some of the main decisions you will need to make step by step.

Decision #1: Fund Type (Hedge, Private Equity, Real Estate)

What type of fund will you need to create? This usually depends on one question. How liquid are the investments? Private funds that invest in marketable securities such as equities, bonds, options, futures, etc., are hedge funds. For investments in private companies that are relatively illiquid, we will classify those as private equity. And real estate — well, that is self-explanatory.

Fund Type	Security Types	Valuation	Redemptions	Subscriptions
Hedge	Marketable Securities	Monthly	Lock-Up Period/Notice Period	100% of investment due upon subscription
Private Equity	Private Debt or Equity Securities	Quarterly	No Redemptions Until Fund Termination	Capital Call Structure
Real Estate	Real Estate-Based Securities	Monthly/ Quarterly	Varies	Varies

Decision #2: Entity Type

It is important to consider the entity type. This will determine in part what types of protections are afforded to the adviser and investors. The most common type of structure for private funds industry-wide is a limited partnership, hence the common reference to LPs or limited partners, who are the investors in the fund. The most popular vehicle for our adviser sponsors at Alta Trust is the business trust. While a private fund may be structured as a corporation or limited liability company, I will limit my discussion of entities here to limited partnerships and business trusts.

Limited Partnerships

The limited partnership structure allows for a general partner to have significant control over the business. The general partner can make most decisions on behalf of the partnership. The limited partners are restricted from actively participating in the business. However, depending on how the Limited Partnership Agreement (LPA) is written, the limited partners may have some voting rights. Due to this type of structure, the limited partner liability is capped at the amount of their investment. The general partner, on the other hand, takes on significant personal liability in the event of a bankruptcy or lawsuit because they were in control. To avoid personal liability, most general partners operate under an LLC structure.

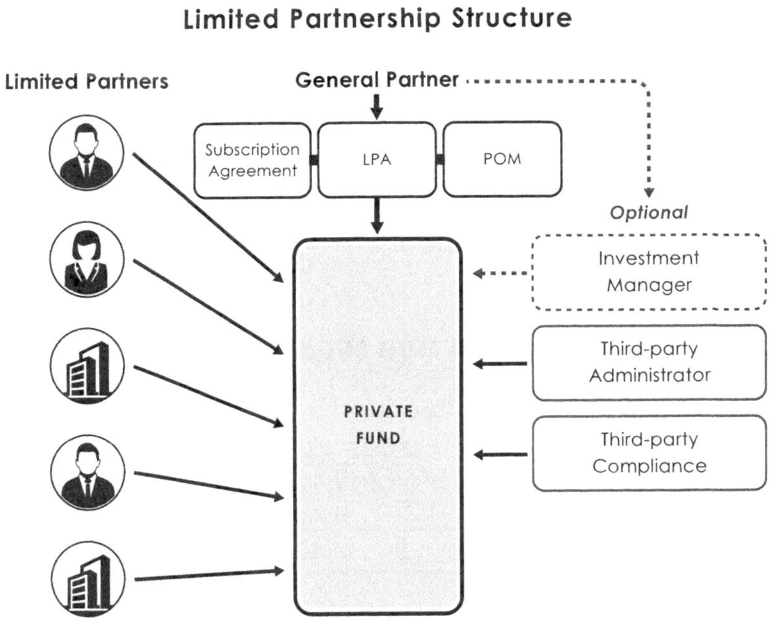

Business Trusts

Statutory business trusts have been around for a long time and are somewhat common in the private fund and mutual fund space. They are often referred to as Massachusetts trusts. They give many of the same liability protections to the sponsor and investors as does a limited partnership, but they also allow for the trust to engage an institutional trustee. The trustee is typically directed by the sponsor (the business trust equivalent of a general partner), but is there to ensure that the assets are accounted for accurately. The documents follow a similar structure, but instead of having an LPA, there is a Trust Agreement.

At Alta Trust, we have taken the role of the trustee in a business trust one step further. Our documents are written to help protect the adviser from taking custody. Investors often like having the additional comfort of a trustee on the fund and sponsors prefer having an additional shield to help them avoid taking custody.

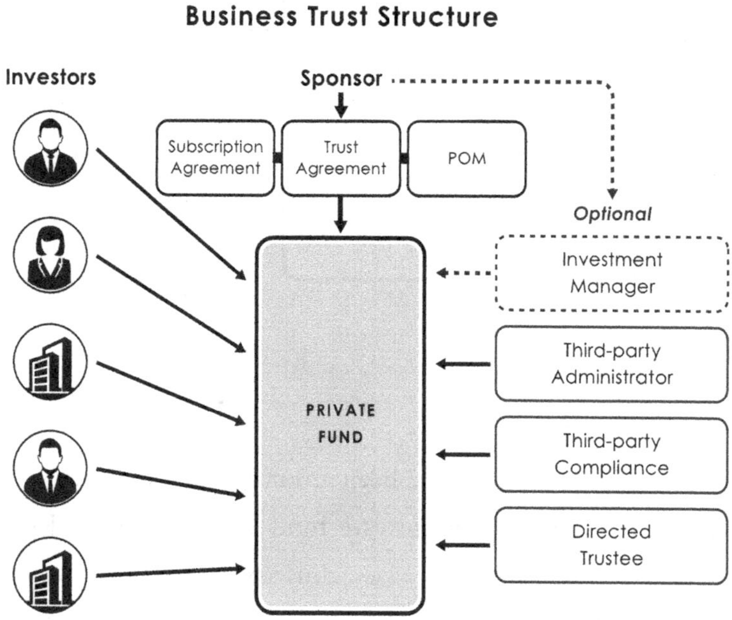

Limited Partnership vs. Business Trust

We are often asked what the difference is between a limited partnership and a business trust. There are three main considerations.

The first revolves around your target investors and their perceptions. Experienced private fund investors will be immediately familiar with a Delaware limited partnership. This is by far the most common type of structure. If you are going for something that is a known quantity, then the limited partnership is a good choice.

The second consideration concerns the RIA. If an RIA is sponsoring a fund, then it needs to be conscious of the SEC custody rules. An RIA as a general partner to a limited partnership will always be deemed to have custody because it has access to the fund assets. At Alta Trust, our business trusts are written such that the adviser is effectively blocked from having access to the fund assets. This, along with a fund audit, helps protect the adviser from having to comply with any burdensome custody rules or custody liability. (*Note: It is possible that the SEC may take a different position on the subject.*)

Finally, many investors really like the idea of having an institutional trustee take custody and help ensure that the fund assets are accounted for. Our advisers use this as a selling point to help attract new investors.

	Limited Partnership	Business Trust
Name of Fund Creator	✓ General Partner	✓ Sponsor
Governing Document	✓ Partnership Agreement	✓ Trust Agreement
Limited Liability Protections	✓ Yes	✓ Yes
Availability	✓ Accredited/ Qualified Purchasers	✓ Accredited/ Qualified Purchasers
Investor Documents	✓ POM/Subscription Agreement	✓ POM/Subscription Agreement
Features	✓ Notice requirements, minimums, share classes, performance fees, etc.	✓ Notice requirements, minimums, share classes, performance fees, etc.
Investment Types	✓ Unrestricted	✓ Unrestricted
Tax Status	✓ Pass-through (K-1)	✓ Pass-through (K-1)
Trustee/ Custodian	✗ No	✓ Yes
Adviser Custody	✗ No Protection	✓ Significant Protection
Common Structure	✓ Very Common	✗ Not As Common

Decision #3: What Will Be the Launch Date?

When will the fund "go live" and be ready to accept subscriptions? This is helpful because it gives you a target to work toward. We usually plan at least eight weeks to launch a fund.

Decision #4: Who Will Be the Sponsor or General Partner?

The main consideration in deciding who will be the sponsor is usually whether the sponsor is a registered investment adviser. If the sponsor is an RIA AND will charge a performance fee, then the suitability standard for investors is "qualified client." This means each investor must meet the threshold of a $2.1 million net worth or $1 million invested with the adviser, as opposed to an "accredited investor" standard of $1 million in net worth or $200,000 in regular annual income.

In some cases, advisers will create a new entity to sponsor the fund and then engage the affiliated RIA as adviser to the fund, in which case they are only paid a standard management fee, while paying the performance allocation to the new sponsoring entity. This approach will allow the fund to keep the accredited investor suitability standard AND charge a performance fee. Make sure to check with your legal counsel to structure this correctly.

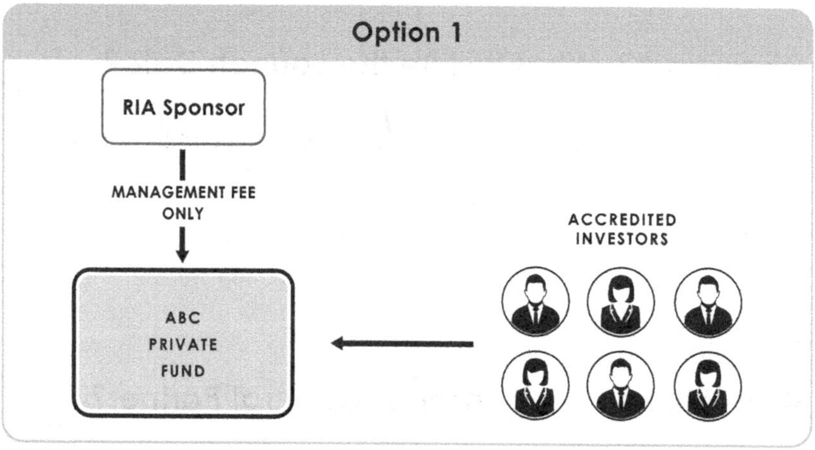
Option 1
RIA Sponsor
MANAGEMENT FEE
ONLY
ABC
PRIVATE
FUND
ACCREDITED
INVESTORS

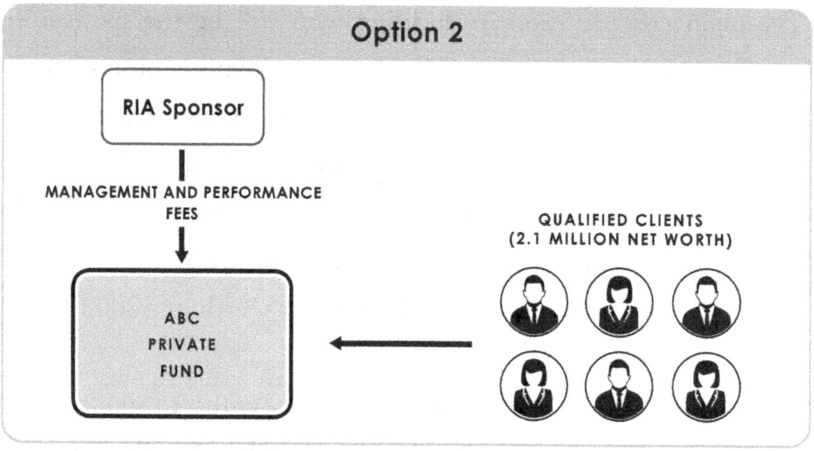
Option 2
RIA Sponsor
MANAGEMENT AND PERFORMANCE
FEES
ABC
PRIVATE
FUND
QUALIFIED CLIENTS
(2.1 MILLION NET WORTH)

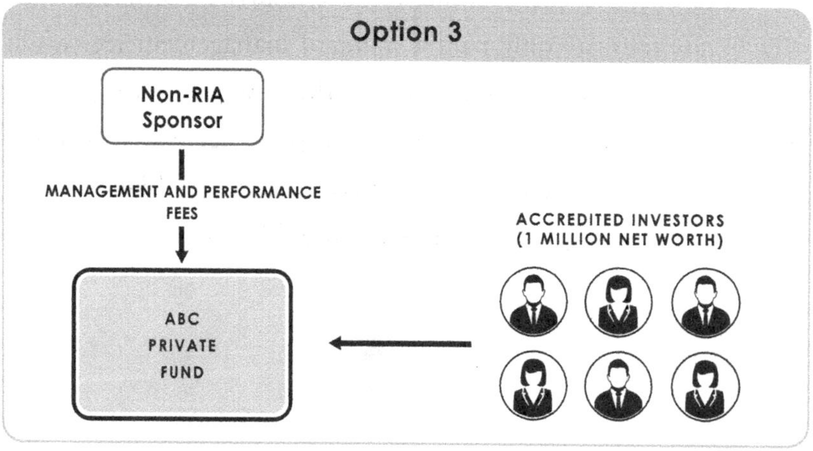
Option 3
Non-RIA
Sponsor
MANAGEMENT AND PERFORMANCE
FEES
ABC
PRIVATE
FUND
ACCREDITED INVESTORS
(1 MILLION NET WORTH)

Decision #5:
Which '40 Act Exemption Will You Use?

You will need to determine which '40 Act exemption you will choose. The exemption you choose will allow the fund to avoid registration with the SEC as a mutual fund, as viewed under section 3c of the '40 Act. We listed the exemptions earlier, but the main exemptions are 3c1 and 3c7 for hedge funds and private equity, and 3c5 for real estate. A 3c1 fund is limited to no more than 100 accredited investors. A 3c7 fund is limited to no more than 2,000 qualified purchasers. A 3c5 fund must invest in real estate and can have an unlimited number of accredited investors. Oil and gas funds may use 3c9, which allows for an unlimited number of accredited investors as well.

Decision #6:
Which '33 Act Exemption Will You Use?

If a fund files an exemption from the '33 Act under Rule 506b, then it is a private offering and only allowed to be discussed one-on-one with known individuals and entities. This is by far the most commonly used '33 Act exemption. For certain funds, a 506c offering makes sense. It is referred to as a general solicitation fund and allows for public marketing of a fund, as long as each investor's accredited investor status is independently verified.

Decision #7: Will the Fund Be Open or Closed?

Will the fund be open for a select period and then closed to new investors or do you want to keep the offering open continuously to new investors? Currently, closed funds are more popular in general, which adds to that element of exclusivity that was discussed earlier.

Decision #8: Will the Fund Have Lock-Up Periods?

Do you want to require an investor to keep their investment for a required length of time? This could be six months, a year or more. It primarily depends on how liquid and marketable the investment strategy is. For the most part, lock-up periods are becoming shorter or disappearing completely in hedge funds. Private equity funds are effectively locked up because there are usually no redemptions for the life of the fund.

Decision #9: What Redemption Rights Will the Investors Have?

Assuming the fund allows for redemptions, how much notice do you need to assure you have enough cash to make the investor liquid? This could vary from 15 days to one year, depending on what the offering documents say. The actual redemption will take place on the next valuation date. For example, if an investor needed to provide 30 days' notice, they would provide the notice on November 30th and the redemption would be booked as of December 31st. Finally, if you have a fund of funds, you need to match up the underlying liquidity with your fund's liquidity, otherwise you could get caught in a pinch.

Decision #10: How Often Will Your Fund Be Valued?

How often do you want to value the fund? Investors receive statements in accordance with each valuation period. Hedge funds are usually valued monthly, and private equity is typically valued quarterly. This also determines how frequently investors can get into or out of a fund if there are redemption rights for investors.

Decision #11: How Will Your Fund Be Valued?

What underlying values will you use to determine the fund's value? Market-based securities are easy to value, but valuation can get more complicated. When it comes to private companies, you may use cost bases, a multiple of EBITDA (earnings before interest, taxes, depreciation, amortization), or an independent valuation. Real estate sometimes uses cost, appraisals or cash flow methodologies to determine the valuation of holdings. In addition to the underlying security values, you will need to add accrued income, liabilities and any corporate actions that might apply for the period. The fund's valuation policy will be explicitly defined in your fund's offering documents.

Decision #12: What Will You Charge?

Management Fees

Determine how much you will charge as a management fee. This is a percentage of assets for hedge funds, usually ranging between 1% and 2%. For private equity funds, the management fee often adjusts based on the stage of the fund (more in the earlier years and less as the fund nears the end of its life), but generally ranges between 1% and 3% annually. Management fees for private equity are based on either committed capital or called capital, and not the value of the fund.

Performance Allocations (Carried Interests)

Are you going to take some of the profits if the fund does well? If so, how much? Will you have a hurdle rate? You should also consider a high-water mark provision (does not typically apply to private equity) that must be met before a performance interest is earned.

Distribution Waterfall

For private equity funds, you need to determine what gets paid to whom and in what order. This is your distribution waterfall.

All the decisions that you just made (and more) will be memorialized in your fund offering and supporting documents.

Fund Documentation

Before going live, you will want to have the following documents in place. It may seem like overkill, but you don't want to be caught without any of the necessary documents. And it's always best to ensure these are prepared prior to the fund launch. Our clients enjoy the benefit of Alta Trust ensuring all these items are taken care of up front.

Limited Partnership Agreement / Trust Agreement

This document lists the duties, powers and authority of each of the parties. It also describes how the partnership or trust will operate and how a variety of scenarios will be handled. This is the core of the structure, and each limited partner agrees to the Partnership Agreement upon subscribing.

Private Offering Memorandum (POM)

The Private Offering Memorandum (POM) is the fund's disclosure document. Some people may tell you that a POM is not necessary (and legally, it is not), but you would be foolish to make any private fund offering without a solid POM. The POM outlines all the players, the structure, the fees and expenses, conflicts of interest, and the risks. This is your insurance policy in case you ever have a complaint or lawsuit. Make sure you go heavy on the disclosures and be very forthright with your investors. Your POM should have a summary section, which will be the most read part of the document. The POM should also cover items such as biographies of the principals, fees, expenses, investment strategy, risks, taxes and any other details that would be important to help an investor make an educated decision to invest in your fund.

Subscription Agreement

The investor signs the Subscription Agreement in order to invest in your fund. By signing, the investor attests to meeting minimum suitability requirements of the fund (i.e., accredited investor, qualified client or qualified purchaser). The investor also attests to receiving and reviewing the POM and accepting the Limited Partnership Agreement or Trust Agreement. The amount of their investment is also detailed, along with any information you will require for background checks before they are admitted into the fund.

EIN

The fund's tax identification number.

Certificate of Trust / LPA Registration

The official registration of the fund with the state of its creation.

Investment Management Agreement

It is a best practice to have the fund sign a Management Agreement with the adviser, even if the investment manager is affiliated with the fund sponsor.

Administration Agreement

This is the agreement between the fund administrator and the fund that details how the fund will be administered. It should reflect the fund's offering documents and include items such as valuation methodology, frequency, reporting requirements, statements, etc.

Compliance Agreement

Whether you contract with a separate third party or do compliance yourself, it is important to have a good program and ensure everything is documented.

Bad Actor Certification

Bad actors, as defined by the SEC, cannot utilize a Rule 506 offering exemption, so this certification documents that Rule 506 can be used. This is an important piece of documentation for every fund. Any "covered person" of the fund should sign a Bad Actor Certification.

Fund Presentation

This is usually a PowerPoint or PDF document explaining the fund, the problem it solves, the value proposition and supporting evidence.

Reg D Filing

Form D needs to be filed for each fund within 15 days of accepting its first subscription.

State / Blue Sky Filings

Each time an investor subscribes into the fund from a new state, the fund must file in that state (typically within 15 days of the subscription).

Key Points

1. Determine what type of fund you want to launch: hedge, private equity or real estate.

2. Which '40 Act exemption will you use: 3c1, 3c7 or 3c5? Each one allows you to raise unlimited amounts of money.

3. Select the specific provisions of your fund in consideration of your investors and your investment strategy.

Exercise: Go through each of the decision points above and see what type of fund you come up with. Determine if it will be attractive to investors.

13

The Alta Trust Private Fund Program

I HOPE YOU ARE EXCITED ABOUT THE PROSPECTS OF MANAGING your own private fund and the world of opportunities that will be opened to you, not to mention the added stature and respect your firm will receive from your clients and in the industry at large. It's normal to be a little intimidated by the regulations and complexities of starting a new private fund.

You've made it this far in the book, so I know you have realized that private funds are an opportunity worth pursuing. In this chapter, you will see how all the complexity we have discussed can become manageable and even simple with the program we have put in place. I'm going to focus on the Alta Trust Private Fund Program because it's what I know and what we have built and, quite frankly, I have never found any other private fund program which even comes close.

We are seeing an explosion of private fund activity. We expect to launch five times more funds this year than last year. Whether you work with us or not, our plan is a proven one and a helpful guide to follow as you move toward launching your brand of funds.

We have spent countless hours meticulously going through every part of the process to make it as efficient and as easy as possible for investors and advisers.

Because the business trust structure is most popular with our adviser clients, I will use it as an example. However, the process is very similar for a partnership structure.

8 Steps to Launching a Private Fund

Once an adviser has engaged Alta Trust, we follow a simple and straightforward 8-step process to launch a fund. Our process ensures that nothing is missed and that every fund launch is successful.

▶ Step 1. Kickoff Call

- ☑ Introductions
- ☑ Review Desired Fund Structure and Provisions
- ☑ Diagram the Fund
- ☑ Set Up the Fund Project Plan

▶ Step 2. Decision Time

- ☑ Determine Fund Name
- ☑ Determine Sponsoring Entity
- ☑ Determine Launch Date

☑ Review Outstanding Questions on Fund Provisions

☑ Draft Offering Documents to be provided to the Sponsor

☑ Establish Virtual Data Room

Step 3. Compliance

☑ KYC/AML Process

☑ Reg D Filing

☑ State/Blue Sky Filings

☑ ERISA Considerations

☑ Investor Count

☑ Distributions

☑ 506b/506c (Fund Solicitation)

☑ Commission Payments

☑ Bad Actor Rules

☑ Data Room

☑ Cybersecurity and Personal Information Handling

Step 4. Offering Documents

The following are reviewed in detail and finalized by the sponsor and their legal counsel:

☑ Trust Agreement

☑ Private Offering Memorandum

☑ Subscription Agreement

▶ Step 5. Operations

- ☑ Trading/Purchase Process
- ☑ Valuation Methodology
- ☑ Valuation Frequency
- ☑ Fee Calculations
- ☑ Sponsor Approvals
- ☑ Establish Fund Operating Account
- ☑ Prime Broker Account (hedge fund)
- ☑ Platforms (reporting)

▶ Step 6. Ancillary Agreements

- ☑ Fund Administration Agreement
- ☑ Sponsor Certificate (approval of offering documents)
- ☑ Investment Management Agreement
- ☑ Certificate of Trust
- ☑ Employer Identification Number

▶ Step 7. Audit / Tax

- ☑ Audit Planning/Process
- ☑ Audit/Tax Engagement
- ☑ K-1 Forms
- ☑ 1099 Forms
- ☑ In-Kind Purchases

▶ Step 8. Subscription Process

- ☑ Manual Process Review
- ☑ Automated Process Review
- ☑ Timing
- ☑ One-off Scenarios

We usually complete one step each week, so that a fund is launched within 60 days. The timeline can be longer or shorter, based on the complexity of the fund or if there is a need to expedite the launch.

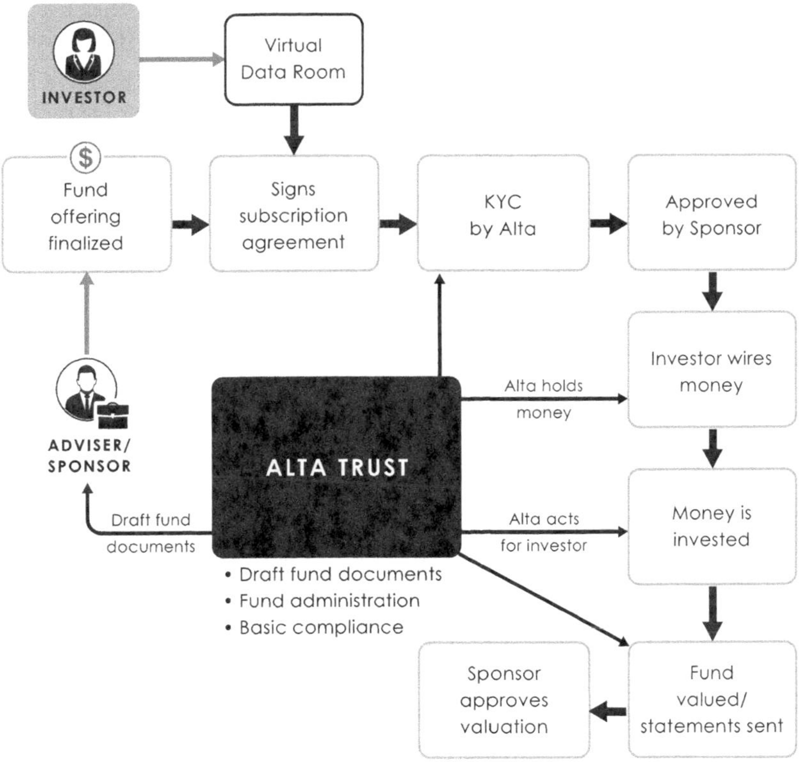

Subscribing Investors

Subscribing investors can be a very cumbersome process. Fortunately, we have an automated system to make it as seamless and simple as possible, while still ensuring that everything is done by the book.

We recommend that all our fund sponsors use a virtual data room to help ensure that goal.

The Virtual Data Room

Not too long ago, and even today, fund sponsors number each POM and keep a handwritten or typed ledger of each prospective investor who received one. You need to understand that these are private investments that must be kept, well, private. If they are offered too broadly, they could be deemed a public offering (unless it is a 506c fund), and the fund would be required to register as a mutual fund. Keeping the ledger is proof that the offering is, in fact, private. Also, sponsors want to control their offering so it remains inaccessible to competitors.

Over the years, email became an easy way to send out fund information. Email is easy to distribute, but impossible for a general partner to control their own documents once they are sent.

A much better way to communicate information about funds has emerged — a virtual data room. It is easy for the sponsor to set up and monitor, and is very secure and convenient for the investors. Most advisers will use a third party that provides these types of services. A virtual "room" is created where the sponsor can store all the fund information that a prospective investor may want to see, such as formation documents, pitch deck, POM, executive biographies, subscription document, etc. The sponsor can invite prospective investors to enter the room by sending them a secure invitation, which will require a passcode for viewing.

Virtual data rooms often have various ways to secure files. With a virtual data room, the general partner can control who sees the fund documents, as well as determine how the investors interact with them.

For instance, there is usually an option to allow the client to download documents, make them "view only," add watermarks, etc. The data room will also keep track of who logs into the site and what documents they view.

Signing Fund Documents

Once the prospective investor is ready to make an investment, they will follow a link to complete a dynamic online form which includes the uploading of a passport or driver's license. The prospective investor then receives a signature-ready document for electronic signature.

Once the Subscription Agreement is signed, we go to work ensuring that the prospective investor meets all of the know your customer (KYC) and anti-money laundering (AML) background checks. Some of these checks include:

- Verify the investor's residence (e.g., LexisNexis, utility bill or other documentation)
- Passport or driver's license
- W-9 form

- Email
- Mobile phone number
- Source of wealth
- Political or celebrity status
- Office of Foreign Assets Control (OFAC) of the U.S. Department of the Treasury check
- Financial Crimes Enforcement Network (FinCEN) of the U.S. Department of Treasury check
- Internet search

Once the KYC/AML check is complete, the sponsor can sign to accept the subscription agreement and the investor will wire the investment to the fund's operating account.

Subscription Process

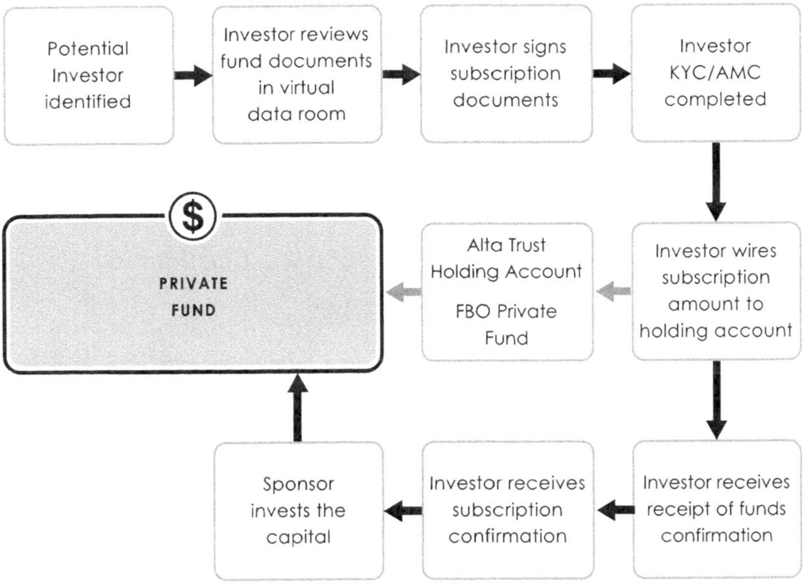

Redemption Process

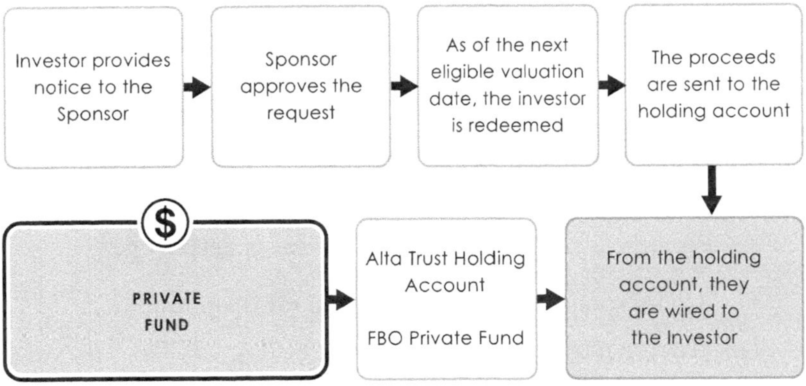

Alta Trust Fund Administration

Once the investor is in the fund, Alta Trust handles all the day-to-day administration work and assists with compliance checks. We handle:

▶ Interest Owner Accounting

- Confirm purchase and redemption confirmations to investors
- Prepare capital call notices
- Track receipt of called capital
- Calculate distributions; prepare and issue distribution notices to investors
- Prepare capital account statements to investors upon each valuation
- Prepare quarterly unaudited financial statements
- Record capital activity of each investor
- Allocate the quarterly fund profit and loss statement to each investor

▶ Fund Accounting

- Record cash flows and reconcile to the general ledger
- Record sponsor-provided valuation for the portfolio investments
- Value the fund in accordance with the organizational and offering documents

- Calculate the preferred return (hurdle rate), if applicable, for the investors, and calculate any performance allocation due to the sponsor
- Administer multiple fee classes, as applicable
- Calculate the distribution waterfall in accordance with the offering documents
- Record expense and management fee accruals and payments
- Record the profit and loss statement of the fund for the quarter and allocate pro rata to the interest owners
- Support annual audit, and prepare draft financial statements with footnotes

Reporting

- Quarterly unaudited financial statements (includes Statement of Assets, Liabilities and Interest Owners' Capital, Schedule of Investments, Statement of Operations, Statement of Changes in Interest Owners' Capital, Statement of Cash Flows)
- Investor Capital Account Statements
- Valuation Reports, for example;
    - Valuation Summary
    - Trial Balance
    - General Ledger
    - Capital Accounts (by investor)
    - Capital Activity (high-level summary)
    - Bank & Cash Reconciliation
    - Portfolio Investments

- Accruals
- Expenses
- Preferred Return (hurdle rate)
- Carried Interest/Performance Allocation
- Quarter-to-date Cost Rollforward
- Year-to-date Cost Rollforward
- Inception-to-date Cost Rollforward

Assistance with Regulatory Compliance

- Prepare and file required federal and state securities notices
- Perform KYC and AML, as well as anti-terrorism checks through government lists such as OFAC and FinCEN
- Monitor the investor count for the fund
- Monitor the fund's ERISA status

The sponsor is left to focus on gathering new assets, managing those assets, and overseeing and approving the work of Alta Trust.

Investors receive regular communications and updates from the sponsor, and Alta Trust provides an online portal where everyone can see their account activity, statements and notices.

Congratulations! You are on your way to launching your first private fund. Yes, there are a lot of details in this book, but I believe you understand what it takes to launch your brand of funds.

So, what are you waiting for? Take the next step. If you are interested in working with Alta Trust, visit **privatefundsmadesimple.com** and set up an initial consultation. I love hearing all the clever ideas our clients come up with to solve challenging problems and provide returns to their clients—all while making a difference in the world.

Whatever you do now, don't let the private fund opportunity pass you by. You have what it takes, and your clients are waiting for the opportunity only you can provide.

Key Points

1. If you are going to sponsor a private fund, you need a system.
2. Make sure you find a partner you can trust.
3. Congratulations on joining the 14% of advisers who see the benefits of private investments and are willing to offer them to their clients.

Conclusion

WE HAVE ALL HEARD THE ADAGE "LUCK IS WHEN PREPARATION meets opportunity." Opportunities present themselves to you every day, but you are prepared to act on new private fund opportunities now.

Private funds are one of the most powerful tools an adviser can have at their disposal. Whether you have a fund with "dry powder" ready to be invested when the deal of a lifetime presents itself or whether you meet a potential partner and know just how to use their expertise, it's time to take the leap.

You are an investment professional who has always been able to identify great investment opportunities in or out of the public markets. Now you are equipped to execute on those opportunities for your benefit and for the benefit of your investors.

I wish you much success in your private fund adventures!

Acknowledgments

IT TURNS OUT THAT WRITING A BOOK IS MUCH HARDER AND MUCH more fulfilling than I could have imagined. I am so grateful for the support of so many to help me write a book that I feel so strongly about.

To my wife, Nicole. I cannot adequately express my thanks for your support and encouragement with this book and always.

To my mom, Cherie Ponder. You always told me that I could do anything and writing this book is something I never thought I would do. Thank you for your support and feedback.

I cannot express enough gratitude to my brother and business partner, Stephen Ponder. Thank you for your constant support and help with this book and always.

Nathan Crisenberry, we weren't born brothers, but over the years we have become brothers. You are the kind of person that I can count on no matter what. Thank you.

I feel so blessed to work with my friends. Aaron Anderson, you have always been a trusted friend and adopted member of the family. Your practical insights for the book were invaluable.

To Fay Matsukage, JD—we met on accident, but it has been a very happy accident for me. I appreciate your knowledge of the law, judgment and sound advice.

Rob Velotta, CPA, MT—reliable tax advice for any private fund solution is essential. Your expertise was critical to get this book right. Thank you.

Mark Pyzdrowski, your deep industry knowledge and accounting expertise made a huge difference in ensuring this book hit the right notes in the right ways.

To Camille Clemmons, a long-time friend and colleague in the industry. I needed your unique perspective and keen eye. I appreciate the time you took to help me.

Bruce Ashton, JD—when it comes to issues of ERISA, you have to get it right. Thank you for always being my "ace in the hole."

To Tom Hall—your time, efforts and intellect were all necessary to create the finished product I had hoped for.

Audrey Howes, you are an exceptional marketer and story teller and you did not disappoint. The readers will be grateful for your recommendations.

Erin Krage, thank you for all of your help moving this project along. It needed to be finished!

Marcy Gardner, the editor of this book and all around amazing lady. I could not have done it without you. You are smart, talented and infectiously enthusiastic. Thank you for persevering.

About the Author

ADAM PONDER, in addition to having managed two private funds, is the co-founder and CEO of Alta Trust Company. He has owned and operated a successful registered investment advisory firm and a retirement plan recordkeeper and third-party administration firm. He lives in Colorado with his wife, Nicole, and their four children. For more information, please visit **www.trustalta.com**.